AF543306

Voluntary Organisation in Third World Countries

Voluntary Organisation in Third World Countries

Dr. Raj Kumar

Neha Publishers & Distributors
Delhi - 110002

Neha Publishers & Distributers
4832/24, Prahlad Gali, S-204, Ansari Road,
Darya Ganj, New Delhi - 110002
Tel. : 23278261, 43570976
E-mail : gauravbookcentre@gmail.com
Website : www.gauravbookcentre.com

© Publishers

Ist Edition, 2011

ISBN : 978-93-80318-06-6

Price : ₹ 895/-

Laser Typesetting by : Tamalika Computers, Delhi

Printed at : Nagri Printers, Delhi-110032

PRINTED IN INDIA

Published by Mrs. S. Chaudhary for Neha Publisher & Distributor, Delhi-110002

Contents

Preface

Voluntary Work for the common good has been the tradition of many countries. But the role of modern state has become complex. Therefore the government has started implementing developmental programmes through the voluntary organizations. How do we define voluntary organisation? Why these organisations started and how they evolved and what is the future of voluntary organisations?

This book, therefore, aims at organising the best material on the subject to suit the needs of students scholars, teachers, NGOs, VOs and general readers. For a global understanding of this issue, we have also included aspects of human rights and international relationship and organisations.

In preparing this book we have incurred indebtedness of authorities on the subject, librarians and their staff members, we respectfully acknowledge them.

Last but not the least, my publisher conceived this project and published this useful material in its present form for wider intellectual persuits and indepth studies, he deserves my readers patronage. We shall feel greatly rewarded, if our readers find the book useful to them.

Introduction

A voluntary organisation is a non-profit organisation formed by a group of voluntary citizens. It may be operating on a local, national or international level.

Commonly called non-governmental organisations (NGOs), voluntary organisations are formed mainly for societal change on a number of issues such as human rights, environment, health, social justice, livelihoods and so on.

Voluntary organisations may work at grassroots level – directly with the communities or may offer some form of expertise and funds to those working at grassroots level. There are various informal voluntary organisations which comprise people who come together to bring about social change at some level. However, a voluntary organisation registered as a legal entity has certain advantages (tax exemption for itself and its donors, better clarity and transparency in accounting to the general public, higher credility, etc.) Such organisations form a part of the organised voluntary sector.

In India, voluntary organisations may be registered as:

1. A Society under The Societies Registration Act, 1860
2. A Trust under The Indian Trusts Act, 1882
3. A Section 25 Company of the Indian Companies Act, 1956

While the bulk of voluntary organisations are registered as any of the above (primarily the first two), some may also be registered as:

4. A Co-operative Society under The Co-operative Societies Act, 1904
5. A Trade Union under The Trade Union Act, 1926

These forms of organisations are more specific in nature and have separate legislations for incorporation. The more commonly found voluntary organisations are:

Societies: which may be engaged in promotion of literature, science, fine arts, spreading knowledge or other charitable purposes.

Trusts: which may have private or public purposes. The purpose of the entity may change in this case under the particular Act used to register the trust eg. The Bombay Public Trust Act, 1950. Under the Indian Trust Act, 1882, a voluntary organisation registered as a Trust must define a public purpose available to a large body of people, with no restriction to a community.

A voluntary organisation may also be registered as a Section 25 company where the directors, promoters or trustees of the company agree that profits are not distributed to them. If voluntary organisations have a higher income than expenditure, the excess is designated as "surplus" not profit. This may be via donations received or from self-generated income. However, unlike companies, voluntary organisations do not distribute this amount, but use it for further programmes.

In general, voluntary organisations are also called

NGOs – Non-Governmental organisations
NPOs – Not for Profit organisations
CSOs – Civil Society Organisations
CBOs – Community Based Organisations
Charitable Organisations
Third Sector Organisations

Some of the work of voluntary organisations may vary over:

1. Advocacy: working on advocacy or campaigning on issues or causes and not implementing programmes.
2. Consultancy/ Research: working on social and developmental research & consultancy
3. Training / Capacity Building: providing training on specific aspects of voluntary work.
4. Networking: bringing together various organisations in a specific field to enable them to work together and share experiences.
5. Grant making and receiving: these organisations receive and disburse funds. They identify specific programmes of other organisations, monitor, evaluate and enable the organisations to execute the programmes.
6. Grassroot level: working directly with the community.

1

Origins of Voluntary Action in India

The roots of voluntary action in India go back in history, Many religious persuasions have been born in India; many others have been nurtured and supported on Indian soil throughout history. One precept which is common to all major religions is that people should work for the well-being of others. All religious scriptures provide guidelines, prescriptions and suggestions for followers to contribute to the well-being of society (Dadrawala, 1991).

Hinduism is the dominant religion in India, practised by over 80 percent of the population. The Hindu concept of which entails a code of moral and social behaviour, including concern for all other human beings, is one of the most important pillars of Hindu Philosophy. There are also several other religions followed by smaller but significant numbers of people; some like Buddhism, Jainism and Sikhism are indigenous and offshoots of Hinduism, while others like Islam and Christianity came from outside. Whatever their religious practice, in every one of them contribution to society is mandatory for their followers. The concept of *dana* (voluntary giving) liar been the cornerstone of the spirit of voluntarism in India.

"A noteworthy feature of all major religions has been the emphasis they placed on charity and sharing wealth with others, especially the poor. In Hinduism, serving the poor is considered equivalent to serving God (Narayan Sewa). Contrary to popular opinion, Hinduism does not have a disdain for worldly pursuits and creating wealth. It is against excessive consumption and attachment to things worldly. In the Bhagawat Gita, which presents the essence of Hindu philosophy. Lord Krishna asks his followers to shun, not right action, but attachment to the fruits of action. In other words, while action is necessary and even liberating, attachment to the fruits of action is enslaving. From this it follows that it is not the creation of wealth (of course by right means) that is to be shunned, but its excessive accumulation and its use for overindulgence. Wealth is believed to have three ends: accumulation, consumption and charity. Of these, charity is considered the best use of wealth followed by consumption and accumulation. Other religions too place an equal emphasis on charity. Helping the needyis generally viewed as the supreme duty of the individual. Buddhism prescribes an elaborate code of conduct for its followers based on the principle of the golden mean-avoiding all extremes. Like Hinduism, it does not frown on creation of wealth but on excessive consumption, arguing for moderation in all activities. It niakes alms-giving obligatory for all its followers. As ail organised religion, it used the institution of the *Sangha* to provide service to the poor. In Islam, charity took the obligatory form of *Zakal* enjoined upon all Muslims. In order to discharge their *Zakat* obligations, all Muslims are required to earmark a part of their income to help the poor and the needy" (PRIA, 2001b: 22).

Helping the poor and the needy, providing for the wellbeing of others; making contributions to society, are values deeply ingrained among people belonging to diverse religions and backgrounds in India. Thus, individual giving and individual acts of service to the needy have, historically, been the main forms of voluntarism in India. These individual initiatives to help the needy thus became the bedrock of voluntary action in India. Institutionalised voluntary action at that time existed mainly within the domain of religious institutions: ashrams and *maths* among Hindus, waqfs and khanqahs among Muslims, and *gurudwaras* and *deras* among Sikhs. Throughout the ancient. and medieval periods, voluntary action-whether individually inspired or collectively supported-found its Vatural expression through religious institutions ill India. Thus, the origins of voluntary action in India go back in history. The form may change over time, but the pursuit of voluntaryaction has continued uninterrupted.

Evolution

In recent Indian history, the most significant and contemporarily relevant form of voluntary action evolved during the 18th and 19th centuries. This period was marked by several stirings for social reform as, under British colonial rule, the influence of modern Western thought began to spread. Ideas of liberty, fraternity and freedom began to influence Indian scholars, thinkers and reformers. It was in this period, therefore, that several initiatives for social reform were born.

The reform movement found its most articulate and inspiring leadership in Raja Ram-mohan Roy the early.19th century. His work in Bengal influenced voluntary work in other regions of the country. Raja Ram-mohan Roy founded the Brahmo Samaj in 1828 with the clear aim of bringing about social, political and economic change in India. As a modern form of voluntary action, it inspired a large number of educated and concerned Indians to work towards eradication of various social evils then prevalent in India, like child marriage and sati.

“The spirit of reform beginning with the efforts of Raja Ram-mohan Roy in Bengal embraced almost the whole of India. Apart from the Brahmo Samaj, which had branches in several parts of the country, the Paramhansa Mandali and the Prarthana Samaj in western India and the Arya Samaj in north India were some of the other important movements among the Hindus. The Prarthana Samaj (prayer society) as an important offshoot of the Brahmo Samaj of Rammohan Roy was started under the leadership of Justice Mahadev Govind Ranade in Bombay in 1867. It was also greatly influenced by the well known contemporary social reformer, Keshab Chandra Sen. The organisation had four avowed objectives: to oppose the caste system, to encourage widow remarriage, to encourage female education, and to abolish child marriage.

With almost similar objectives, the Dev Samaj was established in Punjab in 1887 by Dev Atma" (PRIA, 2001b:6). The influence of the reform movement spread. In the north, the Ahmediva movement in Aligarh, the Kayastha Sangh in UP, and the Sarin Sabha in Punjab are further illustrations of similar efforts to gather people to collectively address social reforms. in Maharashtra, under the leadership of Mahatma Jyotiba Phule, the Satya Shodhak Samaj was founded in 1873. Equality of gender and education for dalits (untouchables) was the hallmark of Mahatma Phule's work. While religious inspiration continued to guide the bulk of the social reform movement, its essential inspiration was humanist, modified in the context of influences coming from the Christian missionaries and Western thought.

"In the 1880s, the Arya Samaj made spectacular advances, particularly in north India under the leadership of Swami Dayanand Saraswati. It achieved great success perhaps because of its very ambiguity, for it combined sharp criticism of many existing Hindu practices (idolatry and polytheism, child-marriage, the taboos on widow remarriage and foreign travel, Brahmin dominance and the multiplicity of castes based on birth alone) with an extremely aggressive assertion of the superiority of purified Hinduism based on

Vedic infallibility over all other faiths-Christianity, Islam and Sikhism. The Arya Samaj soon overshadowed other streams in the contest for the loyalties of reform-minded educated young men of northern India" (PRIA, 2001b:7).

Another interesting feature of this period was the rise of literary associations as well as indigenous newspapers and periodicals. Literary institutions like the Royal Asiatic Society and the Gyan Prakash Sabha were formed around the 1830s. Periodicals like *Darpan* (1832), *Digdarshan* (1840), *Prabhakar* (1841), *Dnyanoday* (1842) and *Dnyanaprakash* (1849) were established in Maharashtra. In Bengal, *Sarnachar Darpan, Sambad 'Prauakar, Tattwabodhini Patrika* emerged around the same time. These periodicals supported the social reform movement and the ideas of freedom, dignity and liberty it enshrined. They also served to bring together people with common objectives, ideas and pursuits, transcending physical and cultural distances during a period of limited communication facilities in India. By the turn of the 20th century, a large number of social reform institutions had been stablished in different parts of the country.

"Voluntary samitis (associations) and organisations proliferated in Swadeshi Movement Bengal in bewildering number and variety. They organised efforts to promote selfhelp in economic and social life, and the development of samitis with a wide range of activities. In 1905 the three leading organisations in the field were the British Indian Association, the Bengal Landholders' Association, and the Indian Association. District Associations were set up in many districts of West Bengal, which called for self-help and sustained social and political work through village associations. They promoted swadeshi industries and agriculture, national education, arbitration courts, cooperative banks, community grain stores and sanitation measures in the villages" (PRIA, 2001b:12).

These were the vehicles for systematising and collectivising voluntary action primarily aimed at reforming the Indian society. Their establishment became so widespread that, to provide a basis for legal registration and incorporation of such voluntary associations, the British Indian Government enacted the Societies Registration Act, 1860. This significant piece of legislation has governed the incorporation of voluntary organisations in India since then.

Freedom Struggle

The first half of the 20th century was marked by a major shift in the manner in which voluntary action operated in India. While several forms of nationalist struggle had evolved in the late 19th century with the formation of the Indian National Congress in 1885 and other such organisations, it was only in the early 20th century that voluntary action received a new thrust. As social reform movements began to gather steam in the late 19th 'century, several leaders began to develop systematic and nationalist critiques of British colonial rule. Dadabhai Naoroji, Sir Pherozeshah Mehta, Gopal Krishna Gokhale, and R.C. Dutt were the pioneers. The Indian National Congress became a platform for articulation of these critiques. In 1905, a mass-based movement against British rule, the 'Swadeshi Movement' was launched in Bengal to protest the decision to partition the then Bengal Presidency. This led to an enormous nationalist upsurge. Voluntary action attained a new dimension of collective effort aimed at overthrowing British rule.

Mahatma Gandhi's entry into the Indian freedom movement during the second decade of the 20th century transformed the nature of this voluntary action in a significant way. He established the Sabarmati Ashram at Ahmedabad in 1916, launched the Champaran Satyagrah in 1917, and the Ahmedabad mill strike in 1918. His signal contribution towards mobilisation of rural masses and the peasantry alongside the industrial working class was at the core of the mass-based voluntary action he launched against British colonial rule. In the early 1920s, he emphasised the need for sustained constructive work, thus combining political resistance to British rule with direct social service. Elements of constructive social work included education, sanitation, protection and promotion of khadi and village industries to help local handicrafts and artisans, and the fight against untouchability, illiteracy and consumption of liquor. People were mobilised in their thousands under Gandhi's inspiring leadership to dedicate themselves to constructive social work in different parts of the country. This was a new form of voluntary action, which combined political struggle for independence with direct constructive work among deprived and poor communities in rural and urban areas.

When Gandhi moved his ashram to Sevagram in Wardha, he began to focus on 'Basic Education' (Nayi Talim). In response to his call, a number as voluntary workers dedicated themselves to the promotion of literacy and basic education in different parts of the country.

"Gandhi introduced a 'constructive programme' to make villages self-sufficient by encouraging people to use the spinning wheel *(charka),* hand-woven cloth *(khadi),* and village industries (gramodyog). During the freedom struggle, dedicated workers undertook Gandhi's constructive programme in the villages. Besides rural development, Gandhi called upon volunteers to participate in India's independence movement' (Sell, 2000: 59).

Another interesting feature of this period was the dynamism and vibrancy of women's leadership in voluntary action. Mahatma Gandhi's call for constructive work inspired a number of women leaders to organise women's groups and associations in different regions of the country. Or Annie

Besant organised such a women's association in Madras in 1917 which became a model for others.

Social reform aimed at improving the status of women was added to the agenda of voluntary action in this period through campaigns in Bihar in 1928 against the *purdah* system and demanding the raising of the minimum age of marriage of girls to 16. This was a significant development, an advance on the earlier period, which transformed the nature of voluntary action in modern India: the mass involvement of rural and urban poor in voluntary action was an important aspect; the linkage between political action and constructive social work was another significant dimension; the enhanced role and leadership of women was a third significant feature of the advances achieved in this period of voluntary action.

National Reconstruction

Immediately after independence was established, attention was focused on national reconstruction, and economic development became a major concern of the government. The Constitution which was adopted in 1951 provided wide scope for the government to function in welfare areas. Most leading activists of the freedom movement joined the government in various capacities and began to work towards the establishment of a new social, economic and political order in the country. As a result, the '50s saw a decline in the favour for voluntary action. Some Gandhian voluntary associations like the Gandhi Ashrams and Sarvoday Samitis continued their activities; many others were taken over by the state either directly or through funding and control over the appointment and functioning of their governing bodies. In the '50s the government set-up the Khadi and Village Industries Corporation (KVIC) and the Central Social Welfare Board (CSWB) to fund the activities of voluntary associations.

However, while social reform activities continued through the new institutions, and while several rural development institutions and schools of social work were established in the early years of independence, to assist the continuation of the pre-independence forms of voluntary action, the state also set-about to create, fund and control a large number of organisations in the fields of the performing arts, culture, music and literature. Whatever the original intentions concerning their 'autonomy', these institutions began to slowly but surely evolve as para-state institutions as the spirit of voluntarism declined. Likewise, the cooperative movement was governmentalised through systematic financing and control over these independent voluntary associations.

By the late '60s, the model of development adopted by the new nation-state began to show signs of malfunctioning. Large sections of the population remained poor; a new class of government servants and government institutions came into being; the bulk of the rural, tribal and dalit populations failed to garner any benefits from the government's development and welfare programmes and policies.

This failure of the government and government.-sponsored programmes to achieve their proposed objectives, especially in relation to the poorest of the poor, provoked stirrings of protest against state policies and mass movements championing the cause of the downtrodden became widespread. The most extreme and militant of these protest movements of that period came to be called the Naxalite movement. The response to the call by Jayaprakash Narayan in 1974 for 'total revolution' evoked an even wider response and led to a significant shift in the age distribution of members of organisations undertaking voluntary action. It mobilised mainly youth and students throughout the country to move beyond dependence on government machinery to initiate reform and to directly participate with the masses in the reconstruction of society. The declaration of a national emergency by Mrs Indira Gandhi in 1975 and the subsequent authoritarian policies and actions of the state contributed to a weakening of this promising transformation in the spirit and nature of voluntary action in independent India.

Development

The post-emergency period could be seen as a new phase of voluntary action in contemporary India-a phase in which development becomes the prime thrust of voluntary associations. This was inspired by an increasing distrust in the capacity and intentions of the nation-state and its agencies to address the real problems of poverty, marginalisation and exclusion in Indian society. This led to a number of new voluntary associations being founded by a new generation of young people who came from educated sections of Indian society. They began to focus on issues of bonded labour, environmental degradation, deforestation, appropriate agricultural technology, literacy, and primary health care. Practically every aspect of human endeavour which was hitherto seen as the exclusive domain of the government and its programmes, now began to be an arena of voluntary action. The bulk of this voluntary action was focused on helping the rural Poor, the tribals and women; some of these activities also spread to urban slums. Issues of housing, human rights, pollution, drinking water and sanitation also became the focus of initiatives by new voluntary associations founded in this period. It also witnessed a new wave of people's movements on issues of environment like the Chipko and anti-dam movements, on rights of women and dalits and minorities.

During the Emergency, Parliament enacted the Foreign Contribution Regulation Act, 1976, (FCRA) for implementation by the Central Ministry of Internal Security. This Act continues to be one of the key problematiques in the relationship between voluntary associations and the state in India. In the early 1980s, the government devised a process of systematic intimidation and harassment of Gandhian voluntary associations which were seen to be supporting the ideas of Jayaprakash Narayan and other opposition leaders of this Period. A commission of inquiry, the Kudal Commission, was appointed to particularly focus on the activities of the Gandhi Smarak Nidhi, the Rashtriya Swayamsevak Sangh (RSS), the Gandhi Peace Foundation and the Association of VoluntaryAgencies for Rural Development. Even during the course of its investigations, this commission did considerable harm to the autonomous and independent status of voluntary associations.

In the 1980s, new institutions for regulating government funding for voluntary associations were established. The Council for Peoples Action and Rural Technology (CAPART), for example was founded in the mid 1980s to channelise funds for rural development and for appropriate technology. In the implementation of various government development schemes and programmes at national and state levels, voluntary associations began to be actively associated on the basis of financial grants to bodies active in the field of rural development-women and children welfare, drinking water supply, adult literacy and environmental issues.

It is in this period that new forms of voluntary association also came into being, though the donunant Society Registration Act of 1860 continued to be the main instrument for incorporation and registration (PRIA, 1987). With the appearance of these new forms of association, this phase of voluntary action began to demonstrate significant advances in capacity and contribution of voluntary associations on a wide variety of development issues. At the same time, individual, informal, community-based voluntary action continued to flourish as disenchantment with the state system of welfare and development began to grow throughout the country. This was also a period when international development organisations (various bilateral and multilateral institutions) began to acknowledge the contribution of voluntary organisations in bringing about sustainable development of communities and societies. This global trend also influenced national policies and programmes, on the one hand, as well as created opportunities for voluntary associations to interact with similar institutions from other parts of the world on the other. This period thus witnessed growing international linkages, exchange of experiences and information and solidarity action by Indian voluntary associations with their counterparts in other regions of the world.

This account of the development of voluntary action in India highlights the changing pattern of voluntary action in India as well as its current form. The overarching purpose of voluntary action is promotion of public good. This common public: good is promoted through individual as well as collective action. Voluntary means of ones own choice, self-chosen, self-determined. Voluntary action is, therefore; self-initiated action to promote some aspect of common public good. This could be the well-being of the community, protection of forests or water harvesting or looking after the animals. Thus the scope of voluntary action is determined by the particular public good that is immediately sought. As is evident. during this period of history, various priorities in the definition of public good were adopted. The roots of voluntary action in India lie, we saw, in religious inspiration and thereby the definition of public good in our period partook of the spiritual throughout. The focus of public good was on social reform in the 19th and 20th centuries. In the early part of the 20th century, political struggle became the primary public good in the form of independence from colonial rule. National reconstruction was the primary focus of public good in independent India. After the period of Emergency, a broader, much more diverse and heterogeneous notion of human development, societal development, became the prime focus of public good. As can be seen during this period the manner of expression of voluntary action also changed. Before the enactment of the Society Registration Act of 1860, most of it was spontaneous, informal and based on traditional religious and cultural institutions. More formal organisations have come into being in recent years. There is a rich and varied mosaic of formations for voluntary action in India today.

2

Voluntary Movement

The UN General Assembly in its 52nd session declared the year 2001 as International Year of Volunteers (IYV). The proclamation of lYV is in recognition to the vital contributions of the volunteers to recognise their achievement in the past to facilitate them for the outstanding work done in the field of volunteerism. To ensure that the full potential contribution of Voluntary Organisations (VOs) is realised, the fullest possible communication and cooperation between national, state & local governments and NonGovernmental Organisations (NGOs) should be promoted in institutions mandated and programmes designed to carry out various schemes. VOs / NGOs need to foster cooperation and communication among themselves to reinforce their effectiveness.

During the nineties, VOs / NGOs have emerged as important players in the development arena. On the one hand, voluntary sector is making significant contributions at the UN sponsored meetings at global level, and on the other, VOs are also working for the empowerment of the poor at the grassroots level and are providing quick help in the management of disasters. Role of VOs was particularly recognised at the United Nations Conference on Environment and Development held at Rio de Janeiro, Brazil in June 1992. Thereafter active presence of VOs continued at all important global international fora, such as the Cairo Population Conference 1994, the Copenhagen World Summit on Social Development 1995, the Beijing Conference on Women 1995, and so on. In the coming years, it is expected that voluntary sector would be playing significant role not only in social sectors but also in other sectors.

Keeping in view the respect for the independence of VOs and their significant role, the emerging voluntary sector is also known as independent sector, third sector, civil-society sector or social economy sector. To recognise the important contributions made by the voluntary sector and facilitate its functioning further in the Tenth Plan this Steering Committee was constituted as per the Planning Commission OM dated 5t" February 2001 (Annexure-I). In this report, after providing an overview of the depth and diversity of voluntary sector in the country, reviewing its recognition in various plans, listing the issues & concerns which lead to the terms of reference of the Steering Committee, recommendations for facilitating and improving the working of voluntary sector are provided.

Voluntarism in India

India has a rich tradition of voluntary action. Before Independence, VOs imbued with the Gandhian philosophy were playing significant role mainly in social welfare activities and now, the range of spheres covered by voluntary sector has expanded considerably covering almost all development related activities. Some of the reasons put forward for increase in the number and activities of VOs are the decline of socialism and an increased national and international funding for voluntary sector. In a number of developmental activities, VOs are working as supplements or complements to the governmental efforts.

Traditionally, NGOs are known as Voluntary Organisations (VOs or VOLOGs) & Voluntary Agencies (VAs or VOLAGs) and recently as Voluntary Development Organisations (VDOs) or Non-Governmental Development Organisations (NGDOs). There are equivalent names for NGOs available in different Indian languages; like in Hindi NGOs are called *Swayamsevi Sansthayen* or *Swayamsevi Sangathan.*

The origin and development of the voluntary sector in India has been shaped by two major influences: one rooted in indigenous traditions and value-systems, and the other a product of the interface between the Indian society and the western world. The Indian traditions and value-systems are in turn rooted in religion that prescribes a code of ethics for the individual and the principles governing social life. A noteworthy feature of all major religions has been the emphasis they place on charity and sharing wealth with others, especially the poor. In Hinduism serving the poor is considered equivalent to serving God. Philanthropy and individual acts of social service have, historically, been the main forms of voluntary activity in India. Institutionalised social service activities existed largely within the domain of religious institutions: *Ashramas* and *Maths* among Hindus, *Waqfs* and *Khanqahs* among Muslims and *Gurudwaras* and *Deras* among Sikhs. Throughout the ancient and medieval periods, voluntary activity - whether individual inspired or state supported - found its natural expression through religions institutions.

The concept of secular voluntary activity accelerated with the advent of western, mainly British, influence in India. The work of Christian missionaries in the field of education and health care, especially in remote tribal areas, stood out as examples of dedicated service to the poor, even though the motivation may have been to win over these people to Christianity. The example of Christian missionary work exerted a great influence on the new English educated elite that emerged in the eighteenth and nineteenth centuries.

The organized form of charity and service to the poor practiced by the Christian missionaries impressed many who tried to emulate them. The activities of the *Brahmo Samaj* in Bengal, *Arya Samaj* in north India and the Ramakrishna Mission in different parts of the country are noteworthy. Mahatma Gandhi further developed the tradition set by these early voluntary religious organizations. Though religious in form, the content of Gandhi's programme was secular: spinning, promotion of cottage industries, decentralization of power and an economy based on the satisfaction of need rather than greed.

After the Independence, there was awareness that development to be meaningful requires mobilisation of resources, public cooperation and creation of social capital. Gradually, professionals from various disciplines joined the voluntary sector to undertake multi-sectoral development work. It has been recognised that no development strategy can be successful unless a shared vision of public sector, private sector and voluntary sector is created and the civil society, having VOs as the key actors, can play a vital role in this strategy for development. The process of social mobilisation and development of people's initiatives cannot be achieved without the active support and involvement of VOs. Therefore, in the Tenth Plan efforts would be made to remove roadblocks and irritants to the growth of voluntary action, which has deep roots in the country.

Diversity of the Voluntary Sector

In India, societies, associations, organisations, trusts or companies registered under the Societies Registration Act, 1860; the Indian Trusts Act, 1882; the Charitable & Religious Trusts Act, 1920 or as a charitable company under Section 25 of the Companies Act, 1956 are considered as VOs / NGOs. In addition, there are informal groups working at grassroots level without being registered under any legislation but may also be considered as part of voluntary sector. VOs may be working in the field of welfare of disabled; development of other disadvantaged sections like SCs/STs, children & women in education; environment; human rights; and on issues like resettlement & rehabilitation of ousters by big projects, right to information and so on. VOs may take up issues concerning a particular village or a community to the global issues like impact of WTO or global warming. The range of associations or societies may vary from a resident welfare association to an advocacy organisation. The substantive areas of work of VOs have changed considerably over time. Recently, in an exercise to map the diversity of voluntary sector in India, Rajesh Tandon (2001) has provided the following typology of civil society associations.

(i) *Traditional Associations*

Such associations exist around a social unit either defined by a tribe, ethnicity or caste. Associations of this variety undertake a wide range of functions in the lives of those citizens. Besides mediating inter-family relations, such associations develop elaborate systems, norms and procedures for governing the use and protection of natural resources. Several important struggles to protect and advance customary rights of tribals over natural resources in different parts of the country have been led by such associations.

(ii) *Religious Associations*

Over the centuries, new facts and religions were born and incorporated into Indian life. Buddhism, Jainism, Sikhism and many other variations challenged Hinduism, Judaism, Christianity and Islam for reform and renewal. Charity, help to the needy, service to the poor and *daan* (giving) have been uniformly recommended by all these religions and sects in India. Education, health care, drinking water, afforestation, social welfare, etc. are numerous arenas of human action where fairly organized forms of civil society activity are carried out by religiously inspired VOs.

(iii) *Social Movements*

In the contemporary Indian context, a number of social movements, spearheaded by social movement organisations (SMOs) have emerged as major manifestations of civil society. These movements are of several types:

- Focusing on the interest and aspirations of particular groups such as: SCs, STs and women.
- Protests against social evils like: liquor, dowry, inheritance rights etc.
- Protests against displacement due to big development projects.
- Campaigns against environmental degradation, corruption and for rights to information, education and livelihood.

VOs / NGOs through these social movements try to reform society, institutions and governance and act as harbingers of social change.

(iv) *Membership Associations*

Membership organisations may be representational - set up to represent the opinions and interest of a particular category of citizens e.g. unions of rural labour, farm workers, women workers, consumer associations etc., professional - formed around a particular occupation or profession e.g. association of lawyers, teachers, engineers, managers, journalists etc., social-cultural - organised around a social or cultural purposes e.g. *Nehru Yuvak Kendras,* clubs for sports, *Natak Mandalis* etc. and self-help groups - a growing category of membership organisations e.g. savings and credit groups etc.

(v) *Intermediary Associations*

These associations function between individual citizens and macro state institutions like the bureaucracy, judiciary and police etc. These could be of several types, e.g. service delivery, mobilizational, support, philanthropic, advocacy and network.

In another well-known classification describing diversity of voluntary sector, David Korten (1990) had proposed four generations of NGOs. Nowadays, NGOs working for peace or conflict resolution or as track-II negotiators between states/nations, international NGOs acting on behalf of the global civil society and conducting research on voluntary sector contributions may be regarded as belonging to the category of Fifth Generation. The Four Generations of NGOs as proposed by Korten are shown in the table below.

Diversity of the activities of voluntary sector can be gauged from large number of schemes being implemented through VOs by various Ministries / Departments. It is estimated that there are about 250 such schemes under operation of more than 20 Ministries / Departments. A list of schemes for voluntary sector of some of the Ministries / Departments may be seen at Annexure-II.

RECOGNITION OF VOLUNTARY SECTOR IN THE FIVE-YEAR PLANS

The voluntary sector has been given due importance in the planning process right from the First Five Year Plan, as emphasis was given on public cooperation in national development with the help of VOs. It was highlighted in the First Plan document that the "Public cooperation and public opinion constitute the principal force and sanction behind planning. A democracy working for social ends has to base itself on the willing assent of the people and not the coercive power of the State." In the Second Plan, it was reiterated that public cooperation and public opinion constitute the principal force and sanction behind India's approach to planning. It was observed that wherever the people, especially in rural areas, have been approached, they have responded with eagerness. In national extension and

Strategies of development-oriented NGOs: Four Generations

	Generation			
	First (Relief and Welfare)	Second (Community Development)	Third (Sustainable Systems Development)	Fourth (People's Movements)
Problem Definition	Shortage	Local inertia	Institutional and policy constraints	Inadequate mobilizing visions
Time Frame	Immediate	Project life	10-20 Years	Indefinite future
Scope	Individual or family	Neighbourhood of village	Region or nation	National or global
Chief Actors	NGO	NGO plus community	All relevant public and private institutions	Loosely defined networks of people and organizations
NGO Role	Doer	Mobilizer	Catalyst	Activist / educator
Management Orientation	Logistics management	Project management	Strategic management	Coalescing and energizing self-managing networks
Development Education	Starving children	Community self-help	Constraining policies and institutions	Spaceship Earth

community project areas, in local development works, in *shramdan,* in social welfare extension projects and in the work of voluntary organisations, there has always been willingness and enthusiasm on the part of the people to contribute in labour and local resources have been made freely available.

The Third Five Year Plan emphasised that "The concept of public cooperation is related to the much larger sphere of voluntary action in which the initiative and organisational responsibility rest completely with the people and their leaders, and does not rely on legal sanctions or the power of the State for achieving its aims. It was realised that so vast are the unsatisfied needs of the people that all the investments in the public and private sectors together can only make a limited provision for them. Properly organised voluntary effort may go for towards augmenting the facilities available to the community for helping the weakest to a somewhat better life. The wherewithal for this has to come from time, energy and other resources of millions of people for whom VOs can find constructive channels suited to the varying conditions in the country." During the Fourth and Fifth Plan, the thrust on public cooperation and involvement of people's organisation was lost due to attack on over territory and recession that followed. During this period investment was focussed especially in intensive agricultural programmes.

In the Sixth Five Year Plan, the idea of participation of people's organisations was again recognised. Success stories in the field, of VOs like the Jamkhed Project on child and health care in Maharashtra, Bharat Agro Industries Foundation's work in animal husbandry and social forestry and Self-Employed Women's Association (SEWA) were quoted and it was stated that the country is dotted with numerous examples of highly successful voluntary action of this nature.

Role of VOs in development got a further fillip in the Seventh Five Year Plan where it was declared that serious efforts would be made to involve VOs in various development programmes to supplement the government efforts to offer the rural poor choices and alternatives. The emphasis continued till the ongoing Ninth Plan, wherein efforts are being made to promote peoples' participatory bodies like Panchayati Raj Institutions (PRIs), Self-help Groups and NGOs for development. The following criteria were identified for identifying voluntary agencies for enlisting help in relation to the rural development programmes:

(i) The organisation should be a legal entity.

(ii) It should be based in a rural area and be working there for a minimum of three years.

(iii) It should have broad-based objectives serving the social and economic needs of the community as a whole and mainly the weaker sections. It must not work for profit but on 'no profit and no loss basis'.

(iv) Its activities should be open to all citizens of India irrespective of religion, caste, creed, sex or race.

(v) It should have the necessary flexibility, professional competence and organisational skills to implement programmes.

(vi) Its office bearers should not be elected members of any political party.

(vii) It declares that it will adopt constitutional and non-violent means for rural development purposes.

(viii) It is committed to secular and democratic concepts and methods of functioning.

In the Eight Plan Document, due emphasis was given on building up people's institutions. It was admitted that developmental activities undertaken with people's active participation have a greater chance of success and can also be more cost-effective as compared to the development activities undertaken by the Government where people become passive observers. It was admitted that a lot in the area of education (especially literacy), health, family planning, land improvement, efficient land use, minor irrigation, watershed management, recovery of wastelands, a forestation, animal husbandry, dairy, fisheries and sericulture etc. could be achieved by creating people's institutions accountable to the community. Therefore the focus of attention will be on developing multiple institutional options for improving the delivery systems by using the vast potential of the voluntary sector.

In the Ninth Five Year Plan, it was admitted that private initiative, whether individual collective or community based, forms the essence the development strategy articulated in the Plan and efforts to be made to remove disadvantages which had prevented some segment of our society in participating effectively in the development process. Keeping up with this line of thinking, "promoting and developing people's participatory bodies like Panchayati Raj Institutions, cooperatives and self-help groups" was one of the objectives of the Ninth Plan.

The Mid-Term Review (MTR) of the Ninth Five Year Plan (October 2000) has also documented some successful and sustainable projects undertaken by VOs and other people's organisations. The MTR has identified following problems in the performance of Central and State Plans. Some of these maladies faced by the country can be mitigated by the emerging voluntary sector as a compliment and supplement to the State efforts.

- The critical factor appears to be effective governance to ensure balanced growth of the different regions of India.
- Development is an outcome of efficient institutions rather than the other way around. There is a need to focus on building institutions and improving governance from maximising the quantity of development funding to maximising of development outcomes and effectiveness and efficiency of public service delivery."

Further, under the 'Directions for Reforms' of MTR, it has been inter-alia suggested that "Initiatives by local bodies,

NGOs and women need to be encouraged", to resolve some of the above-referred problems.

It has been observed in the Approach Paper to the Tenth Plan that in many states, we have: hospitals / dispensaries but absence of personnel and there are school buildings but teachers remain absent. To rectify these anomalies and to achieve most of the targets set up for the Tenth Plan, the need to promote voluntary sector has been recognised. The theme of encouragement to voluntary sector continued in the Approach Paper to the Tenth Plan and reflected in the following words, "In view of the continued importance of public action in our development process, increasing the efficiency of public interventions must also take high priority". The minimum agenda proposed in the Approach Paper has recognised voluntary sector by putting "greater decentralisation to PRIs and other people's organisations" as one of the items for the Tenth Plan.

The voluntary sector deserves encouragement to ameliorate at least some of the above-referred problems, because of its following comparative advantages:

- VOs / NGOs are much closer to the poorer & disadvantaged sections of the society.
- Staff of VOs is normally highly motivated and altruistic in their behaviour.
- VOs can easily stimulate and mobilise community resources and have access to volunteers.
- They are more effective in bringing people's participation.
- VOs are less rule-bound and are non-bureaucratic, non-formal and flexible in their structure and operations.
- Voluntary sector has greater potential for innovations.
- VOs prefer to work in a multi-sectoral framework.
- VOs are catalysts for creating social cohesion (Kumar 1998).

Certain disadvantages or shortcomings of voluntary sector are also well known, namely, their inability to cooperate with each other in a way which would allow for coherent policy making, their accountability & transparency is not perfect and their operations are smaller in scale. Therefore, there is a need to improvise the working of VOs by scaling up their operations and by malting them transparent and accountable.

Role of Planning Commission vis-a-vis Voluntary Sector in India

To create an enabling environment for the voluntary sector to collaborate with Government for development, a number of steps have been taken by the Government of India during the year 2000. The most significant step taken by the Government of India, in March 2000, was to declare the Planning Commission as the nodal agency for the GO-VOs interface. This was a step needed to have a focal point from where an integrated and holistic view on the voluntary sector could be taken. As a nodal agency, the first task assigned to the Planning Commission is to create a database on VOs. On the website of Planning Commission, now we have information on about 13,000 VOs / NGOs who have received grants from different Departments / Ministries. In addition, information on about 1,000 VOs perceived by various bilateral, multilateral, intermediary and governmental agencies as good / valid VOs / NGOs is also available at the Planning Commission. website. The NGO database of Planning Commission is continuously being updated.

APPROACH TO THE TENTH PLAN

As mentioned earlier, the Approach Paper to the Tenth Plan has recognised the role of public action, which is best mobilised by the voluntary sector, in the development process. In addition, following paragraphs of the Approach

Paper also recognised and highlighted the importance of voluntary sector.

Population

"The National Population Commission will play a catalytic role in improving centre-state and inter-sectoral coordination, and in involving private sector, voluntary institutions and civil society at large for generating a vigorous people's movement to support the national efforts to achieve the goals set in the National Population Policy 2000."

Corrective Measures

"An important channel for mobilising resources for development, particularly for social sectors, namely the Externally Aided Projects (EAP) and direct funding of projects (i.e. outside budgetary flows) by the NGOs has not been sufficiently integrated with our planning process. Consequently, an important source of scarce resource for development, in the third world context, is not being adequately tapped."

Forests

"The problems and constraints in forestry development include lack of awareness about multiple roles and benefits of forests, especially its role in drought proofing and prevention of soil and water run-off, no linkage between management and livelihood security of the people, low level of technology, inadequate research and extension, weak planning capability, wastage in harvesting and processing, market imperfections, overemphasis on government involvement and control, low level of people's participation and NGOs involvement, lack of private sector participation, unwanted restrictions on felling transport and marketing of forest produce grown by the people, lack of inter-sectoral coordination and weakness and conflicting roles of public forest administration."

Non-Conventional Energy

"There is a significant potential to meet the basic energy requirement of people (viz. cooking & lighting etc.) both in the rural & urban areas, in an economically efficient manner through non-conventional and renewable sources of energy. ... People's participation through Panchayats, other local bodies, co-operatives and NGOs is to be secured in planning and implementation of such programmes."

Governance Reforms

"Review the Official Secrets Act, and supplement it by a Right to Information Act. Rule 9 of the All India Services Conduct Rules and similar other Rules which prevents information from being provided to an ordinary citizen should be deleted, and another rule is added highlighting the intention of the Government in favour of transparency and stating that all such information which is generally provided by the Assembly/Parliament to a Member of Legislature, should also be provided to any member of the public, including NGOs. It must be recognised that improvement in governance would take place only when countervailing forces in society develop confidence to oppose inefficiency and corruption in government. Therefore, in addition to promoting genuine civil society organisations, government should also relax FCRA provisions so that NGOs have easier access to alternative funding."

On the issue of legislations impinging on the functioning of voluntary sector, including the Foreign Contribution Regulation Act (FCRA), Planning Commission set up a Task Force on Laws relating to the Voluntary Sector on 3rd November 2000. The Task Force deliberated on various laws (copy at Annexure-III) in vogue for registration of VOs and suggested inter-alia to change the procedures under FCRA, which are cumbersome, non-transparent and regarded as source of harassment. For promoting genuine civil society organisations (CSOs), VOs / NGOs and other people's organisations (POs), following recommendations are put forward by the Steering Committee on Voluntary Sector for the Tenth Plan.

RECOMMENDATIONS

Simplification of procedures / guidelines for involvement of the VOs / NGOs

Following suggestions for flexible simplified common minimum guidelines are proposed to take care of the contextual and regional ramification in dealing with voluntary sector and keeping in view the diversity of schemes being implemented by various Departments / Ministries. There may be exceptions in any of the specialised scheme due to the special groups or problems to be tackled and there can be variations in the norms for schemes due to different climatic conditions and geographic locations.

(1) The Planning Commission should examine periodically all the issues related to simplification of procedures / guidelines for involvement of the voluntary sector, as an ongoing process. The Annual Plan discussions with Departments / Ministries of the Central Government and with State Governments could be the appropriate fora for such discussions on regular basis. To carry out this responsibility, the Voluntary Action Cell of Planning Commission should be appropriately strengthened.

(2) Information about various schemes for VOs should be widely disseminated. It should be available at the reception office and on the website of all concerned Departments / Ministries. In addition, the information should be published at least once a year in the national dailies and in local newspapers by all the

Departments / Ministries implementing schemes through voluntary sector.

(3) The application form in respect of each scheme should be properly drawn to make it simple and user-friendly and quickly appraisable. A copy of the proposed simplified model proforma may be seen at Annexure-VI for consideration and adoption by concerned Departments / Ministries.

(4) Proposals received from VOs should be acknowledged promptly and preferably an indication given as to the date by which they may expect final decision. Status of the proposal(s) should be available at the reception office and on the website of all concerned Departments / Ministries.

(5) Each Department / Ministry should have a database of all those VOs / NGOs who have availed of funding from them, along with their articles / memorandum of association, etc. Once a VO / NGO has been granted assistance after furnishing information, such as articles / memorandum of association, lists of office bearers / trustees etc. to a Department / Ministry, it need not be necessary for it to file the same information repeatedly year after year (unless there is a change).

(6) Sanctioning system for schemes implemented through voluntary sector may be decentralised. The model of Mother NGOs (MNGOs) adopted by Department of Family Welfare may be adopted by other Departments / Ministries. A designated MNGO or a Nodal NGO may be allowed to take care of the work of three-four related sectors. While adopting the concept of MNGOs care should be taken that it should not hamper the growth of smaller / newer NGOs. Planning Commission should be informed in all cases where funding of more than one crore is provided to any Mother / Nodal NGO.

(7) VOs / NGOs should be shown proper dignity as knowledgeable partners in the development process

and not treated as pawns, contractors or beneficiaries by the staff dealing with the voluntary sector.

(8) The VOs / NGOs look forward for knowledge managers who can sift & sort information for them. In this regard, there is need for funding the NGO networks. Concerned Departments / Ministries may like to formulate schemes to support sector specific networks. CAPART should have a fresh look at its mandate to accommodate a scheme for supporting NGO networks working for integrated development and are of inter-sectoral nature.

(9) Copies of the sanction letter of each scheme / project sanctioned to VOs / NGOs by every Department / Ministry should be endorsed to the District Authority and concerned Department of the State Government. District authorities (may be the District Information Officer) should have information about all NGOs working within their jurisdiction.

(10) Established VOs / NGOs should be treated on fast track or on green channel basis. Priority should be given to innovative schemes and mission driven initiatives of VOs. Procedures for sanctioning projects to new and smaller VOs should be different, compared to the established ones.

(11) For the release of government aid for disaster or emergency relief activities by VOs / NGOs, special assessment and clearance procedures should be adopted to ensure quick and timely support.

(12) Concerned Departments / Ministries may consider limiting the number of projects awarded to a particular VO / NGO depending on its capacity.

(13) Voluntary sector organisations should be allowed freedom of work and all the guidelines should be flexible and it should not be bound by the interference of District or State level committees.

(14) Some flexibility should be given to VOs / NGOs to re-allocate funds under different heads, as per the specific needs and local situations.

(15) As mentioned in the Seventh Plan Document, those VOs / NGOs having affiliations with any political party or those not committed to secular & democratic concepts & values of functioning should not be allowed to get government funding.

(16) The suggestion to provide endowment funds to VOs was appreciated but it was felt that such funds should be raised by VOs themselves from non-governmental sources. However, concerned Departments/ Ministries should consider providing long term grants to established VOs to mitigate the sense of insecurity in terms of sustaining the core activities and staff.

Capacity Building Measures

(1) The concerned Departments / Ministries as well as the State Governments will have to play a key role in capacity building of VOs / NGOs by conceptualising and providing required infrastructure for locally relevant training programmes to the NGO workers.

(2) Simultaneously, training programmes need to be extended to the public officials dealing with voluntary sector, particularly those working in the areas of law & order, judiciary, revenue, forest, etc. with special focus at the grassroots level. State level civil service training institutions should be used for the purpose, involving resource persons from the voluntary sector.

(3) We talk about local resource mobilisation for sustaining the VOs as well as their specific interventions but majority of VOs are not adequately skilled in doing so. Therefore, capacity building needs of the VOs for the complex local resource mobilisation may be met by adequate workshops / trainings. Unless such fund raising capacity is built up, there is no need to reduce the funding of VOs getting support from government by concerned Departments / Ministries.

(4) Some of the areas identified for capacity building of voluntary sector are; service delivery, concept & practice of people's organisations, PRA, GIS, MIS,

gender & development, indigenous resource mobilisation, project formulation, traditional wisdom / indigenous technical knowledge, social audit, multi-stake holder partnership, report writing, communication skills, financial management, monitoring & evaluation, networking & advocacy skills, etc.

(5) Training programmes for the government officials at district, state and centre level should be so designed that the need for bringing about attitudinal changes about the voluntary sector is also taken into account. Focus of the capacity building should not be on tools and techniques but on changing perspectives, motivation and identities.

(6) There should be an inbuilt provision for some amount of funding for training in schemes to be implemented though voluntary sector. While sanctioning bigger projects to VOs, some percentage of grants could be earmarked for capacity building under the heading of training, for enhancement of the capability of the NGO workers.

(7) Capacity building cannot go in piecemeal manner and it has to be a long-term holistic process taking care of the concerns of NGO staff as well as of the organizational capacity. A scheme for deputation of NGO staff to Government and of staff of Central / State Government (administrative & technical) to NGOs may be considered by the concerned Departments / Ministries.

(8) Training programmes run by some NGOs are costly and smaller NGOs cannot bear that cost. Therefore, the Government should take care of training needs of smaller NGOs. A scheme of fellowships for those who cannot afford to undergo training may be launched by concerned Departments / Ministries.

(9) Mother NGOs should be identified and entrusted the role of capacity building of smaller NGOs at the field

level. Mother NGOs may be given charge of managing the work of capacity building in 4-5 related sectors.

(10) VOs / NGOs are generally under-managed; therefore, there is a need to provide inputs from management schools. Already, a Management Institute of Mumbai sends / attaches its management students with reputed NGOs for a period of six weeks. This practice needs to be promoted and replicated in other management schools / institutes.

(11) Steps should be taken to identify capacity building organizations available within the voluntary sector and the government (such as NIPCCD, IIPA, NIHFW, NIRD) and their network could be facilitated by an appropriate government agency. In this regard, the Institute of Applied Manpower Research (IAMR), which is already conducting training / orientation for Young Professionals of CAPART, may take a lead and conduct demand driven training programmes regularly for the workers of VOs / NGOs as well as for the government officials dealing with voluntary sector, separately and in mixed groups.

Partnership between Voluntary Sector, Private Sector & Local Government

(1) Corporate Social Responsibility (CSR) needs to be promoted. To attract corporate funding and partnership with private sector, accrediting or validation of VOs / NGOs and a methodology for that is required. Validation / accreditation of VOs / NGOs would be useful for both private & public sector and international donors. Concerned NGO networks, intermediary organisations and Ministries / Departments may evolve suitable methodologies for the purpose.

(2) Partnership between VOs and PRIs is essential for micro-level development planning. Representatives of voluntary sector be taken on PRI committees / councils and vice versa. *Gram Sabha* and other

stakeholders must be informed of every project and details regarding the project activity & beneficiaries etc. by VOs / NGOs, as well as by the PRIs.

(3) The role of VOs / NGOs as specialised agencies and as a countervailing power, to take care of the public interest is required in tandem with the local-self government.

Promoting / Reviving / Galvanising the spirit of Volunteerism

(1) Successful cases of volunteerism need to be recognised, documented and disseminated appropriately.

(2) To promote the spirit of volunteerism the recurring grant to VOs / NGOs should not exceed 90% of the total funding. VOs / NGOs involving volunteers in their projects should be given preference by the grant-in-aid committees.

(3) Research organisations should measure quantitatively the contribution of volunteering on social and economic development and highlight it at the appropriate forums.

3

Issues of Voluntary Organisation

To provide the enabling environment for promoting and facilitating the work of emerging voluntary sector, the following five issues were taken up for deliberation by the Steering Committee.

Simplification of procedures/guidelines for involvement of the VOs / NGOs

There is a lot of variation in the procedures / guidelines of the departments of the Central and State Governments, and other organisations, for involving VOs in different programmes / schemes. In most cases, Government assistance is available only through straitjacketed schemes. Moreover, most of the departments / ministries have not played a proactive role in establishing partnership with committed VOs and have generally confined their attention to only those who apply for funds to their offices. They have, on their own, not requested good VOs to come to their fold and begin a relationship. Generally, Departments / Ministries subject all proposals including those from good VOs to a uniform appraisal procedure inhibiting sensitive or well-established VOs or those engaged in social activism from approaching the government departments. Generally, it is difficult for the Government machinery to properly examine large number of proposals received from VOs /

NGOs and monitor activities of the sprawling voluntary sector. For monitoring and evaluation, CAPART has a panel of monitors who visit the NGO sites and a system where they have desk appraisal, prefunding appraisal, mid-term appraisal and terminal evaluation. CAPART has decentralised the distribution of funding to NGOs through their regional offices. The Department of Family Welfare under the Reproductive and Child Health (RCH) Programme has identified Mother NGOs (MNGOs) and a Committee selects smaller or field NGOs to work in districts. A list of NGOs receiving grant of one crore or above from CAPART and of MNGOs of Department of Family Welfare are enclosed at Annexure-III & IV respectively.

Suggestions of some of the earlier Government of India reports such as the 'Report of the Expert Group on simplification of procedures dealing with Voluntary Organisations' (1987), 'Action Plan to bring about Collaborative Relationship between Voluntary Organisations and Government' (1994) and 'Study Report on Monitoring of Government Aided NGO Projects' (1997) were considered while discussing the existing methods / procedures for selection of NGOs, release of funds and monitoring of their work, etc. by the Steering Committee. It has been felt that steps need to be taken to make procedures for providing grants to VOs simplified and user friendly.

Capacity Building of the Voluntary Sector

Traditionally, capacity building interventions have focused on strengthening state and public sector institutions. However, due to growing importance of civil society organisations, there is a need now to find ways to strengthen the capacity of these organisations.

Capacity building means development of both individual workers and the organisation. It is essential to focus not only on the individuals in an organisation, but also organisation itself. It is essential to address the issue of institutionalising capacity in an organisation, which is a long term and gradual process (IFCB 2000).

It was recognised that there is a need to build up the capacity of voluntary sector to act as a balancing force between the State and market institutions. Suggestions to make VOs / NGOs more effective for good governance, service delivery and managing newer challenges of development, by providing appropriate training, etc. were thought to be worth discussion by the members of the Steering.Committee.

Facilitating the Inter-Sectoral Partnerships

One of the major challenges facing the world community, as it seeks to replace unsustainable development patterns, is the need to activate a sense of common purpose on behalf of all sectors of society. Forging such partnerships successfully is the emerging new mantra of the new millennium. As discussed above, some steps have been initiated to fortify the collaborative relationship between government and VOs but still a lot has to be done to increase the existing partnership levels between voluntary sector and Private Sector & PRIs / Municipalities. It was felt necessary to explore possible ways to nurture genuine partnerships and dialogue, while recognizing the independent roles, responsibilities and special capacities of each sector.

Reviving / galvanising the spirit of Volunteerism

The UN sponsored International Year of Volunteers - 2001, provides a unique opportunity to highlight the achievements of the millions of volunteers worldwide and to encourage more people globally to engage in volunteer activity. Volunteerism is related to the part time or full time work done by any person on his / her own free will for the welfare and development of people and society. It appears that over the years, increased dependence on the state has reduced the volunteering spirit amongest the people, which needs to be revived.

Monitoring & Evaluation of schemes implemented through Voluntary Sector

Like the existing variations in case of procedures / guidelines of various Departments for seeking proposals from VOs / NGOs, there is a lot of variation in the methodologies adopted for monitoring and evaluation. The concern for proper monitoring and evaluation of the work of voluntary sector has been raised from different quarters. Suggestions were sought to improve the existing methodologies for monitoring and evaluation of the work undertaken by the voluntary sector.

Under this backdrop, following were the terms of reference of the Steering Group on Voluntary Sector:

(1) To review the policies, procedures, guidelines of the government and other organisations for involving voluntary organisations in different programmes / schemes and suggest alternative policies and simplified procedures / guidelines for involvement of the voluntary sector.

(2) To review the existing arrangements for capacity building of the voluntary sector and suggest measures to make VOs / NGOs more effective for good governance, service delivery and managing newer challenges of development.

(3) To examine the existing partnership levels between voluntary sector and private sector & PRIs / Municipalities and recommend appropriate steps to facilitate and enhance such partnerships.

(4) To review the level of people's participation and volunteerism in development programmes and suggest measures for reviving / galvanising the spirit of volunteerism and people's participation in development, particularly, suggesting ways for effectively utilizing services of volunteers, through VOs / NGOs, in the management of disasters such as earthquakes, floods, famines and cyclones etc.

(5) To review the existing methods for monitoring and evaluation of schemes / programmes implemented through VOs / NGOs and suggest improvements in methodologies for effective monitoring and evaluation.

The First Meeting of the Steering Committee was organised on 16.03.2001 with an agenda to solicit the views of the Members on the line of Approach and the Strategy to be adopted in the Tenth Plan to facilitate the emerging role of VOs. The Second Meeting of the Steering Committee was held on 09.06.2001 to discuss the rest of the Terms of Reference of the Committee. Taking into consideration, the conscious decisions arrived at in the two meetings and the recommendations of the other available reports, the Steering Committee finalized its recommendations.

4

Voluntary Action and State

The South Asia region is characterised by the varied forms of State it has evolved since the end of World War II. While India and Sri Lanka have had a parliamentary form of democracy since the early '50s, Pakistan and, later, Bangladesh have lead. long periods of military dictatorship; Nepal and Bhutan remained traditional monarchies. The last decade has witnessed a transition in this regard with the reassertion of democracy in Bangladesh and Nepal. Thus South Asian countries provide a diversity of forms of governance over the past five decades.

The second important dimension of the character of the state in South Asia has been its dominant interventionist role in prornoting development, particularly in India and Sri Lanka. The state took upon itself a pre-eminent and monopolistic stance in defining what constituted 'development', 'public good' and 'national interest' It took upon itself the sole prerogative and the power to control resources, ideas and programmes of development. Thus, in countries like India, there emerged elabo ate development delivery agencies and planning mechanisms in all sectors of human endeavour. This state-led model of development became so pronounced in India that every aspect of human life was controlled or influenced by the agenda set by the state and its agencies. The most critical issue in this regard was the definition of public good and national interest and elaboration of the concepts and programmes of development itself. The state and its operators, in particular its political leadership and its bureaucracy, continued to define their own hegemony over developmental perspectives and programmes and began to feel threatened if alternative ideas were proposed, or a critique of the dominant development paradigm was expressed.

State Roles

Any discussion of relations between voluntary organisations and the state: needs to be based on a thorough understanding of the nature of India's voluntary organisations oil the one hand, and the character of the Indian state, on the other. The Indian state has performed several key roles' in relation to voluntary organisations since independence.

Regulator

One of the functions of the state in a modern society is to regulate the social, political and economic 'spaces. The state enacts a variety of regulatory mechanisms through its organs and agencies as well as through laws and legislations.

Three types of legislation directly affect voluntary organisations in India today. The first relates *registration or in-corporation*. The most common form of registration is as a society or a trust, both under laws enacted under British rule, The Society Act has since been modified and amended by several state governments. In some fundamental ways, incorporation or registration provides a legal identity to voluntary organisations and, therefore, limits the liability of its promoters and founders. But it also entails "playing by the rules of the game" as established by the state, with each successive amendment to the Society Registration Act in different states of the country attempting to further tighten the state's grip on the voluntary organisations by giving unilateral and inordinate powers to the agents of the state to intervene, regulate and check the activities of voluntary organisations registered under the Society Registration Act of those states (PIMA, 1991).

The second set of legislation that affect voluntary organisations are related to. finance. Two specific laws become relevant here. One is the Income Tax Act, 1961, which has always treated the activities of voluntary organisations as being at par with that of business trusts running charitable hospitals, dispensaries, educational institutions, etc. In fact; the Income Tax Act gives special concessions to boarding schools, public schools, hospitals and dispensaries, but not to voluntary organisations engaged in either non-formal adult education pr primary health care. Thus, every year, voluntary organisations must justify their non-profit status in the eyes of the Income Tax Department. Over the years, various amendments to the Income Tax Act have been made with a view to further tightening state control over voluntary organisations, and to create conditions under which the economic viability prautonomy of voluntary organisations is undermined. For example, the current provisions of the Income Tax Act make it impossible for voluntary organisations to carry put any activity to raise resources on their own because surplus genetated through such activities would be liable to tax.

The second law concerning the finances of voluntary organisations is the Foreign Contribution Regulation Act, which was enacted in 1976 during the Emergency. It aimed at regulating the flow of foreign grants and contributions to *all kinds of* voluntary organisations and was located in the Ministry of Internal Security and Home Affairs where those responsible for its implementation treat it as a problem of law and order, and not as a matter related to developmental social change.

In a dramatic amendment to tire Act through an ordinance, first in late 1984 and subsequently by enactment of legislation in January 1985, the Government of India restricted the receipt and utilisation of foreign contribution by voluntary development organisations. The amended Act required old organisations to seek registration with the Ministry of. Internal Security and to provide statements of receipt arid utilisation with audited statements of accounts. The practice over theyears became such that the Ministry of Internal Security re-fused to grant fresh registrations to voluntary organisations. And even tightened the restrictions on them to application; for prior permission to receive foreign contributions. Also,the provisions concerning cancellation of registration numbers arid inquiries under the Act were used selectively by the Ministry of Internal Security to intimidate and obstruct the work of voluntary organisations on such nebulous grounds as "threat to national security" or "public interest". Currently, the Foreign Contribution Regulation Act arid the concerned Ministry implementing it continue to be objects of fear for the vast majority of Indian voluntary organisations.

The Act has been further amended since then with a view to further tightening it in an attempt to limit the space and narrow the work of voluntary organisations. In an overall sense, over the last twenty years. The state has been tightening its grip as a regulator and using its powers more often than not for limiting the space, work and the activities of those types of voluntary organisations which go beyond mere provision of help and charity and the welfare of the poor.

It is ironic that, "In some sense[s], the experience of those managing such [voluntary] organisations today suggests that the legal framework is much more restricting for non-profit sector organisations than for for-profit organisations. The liberalisation of [the] economy and reforms in the 1990s have created greater space, flexibility and ease of operation for forprofit organisations, but very little has changed for non-profit organisations." (PRIA, 2001a: 40)

Funder / Donator

Historically, a very unique role the State has played in India is that of funder of voluntary organisations. Right after independence, the then Congress government began to utilise its access to vast resources to provide land, facilities, infrastructure and funds to a large number of Gandhian organisations to enable them to continue their work as voluntary organisations. In fact, several institutions have been set up by the government over the last fifty years to find ways to promote funding of voluntary organisations. One of the earliest to be set up was the *Khadi and Village Industries Corporation (KVIC)-a* unique institution set up to finance activities of organisations engaged in promoting khadi and village industries for the economic upliftment of the poor, as well as to provide marketing channels and retail outlets for their products.

The *Central Social Welfare Board (CSWB),* and its counterparts in the various states, are another set of unique institutions set up in the late '50s to provide assistance to organisations engaged in social welfare work, particularly the welfare of the poor, the destitute and the weak, with a focus on women. Subsequently, a large number of departments and ministries of the national and state governments began to evolve schemes for funding voluntary organisations. The ones most commonly aided have been in adult education, literacy, health care and, in recent years, in environment protection and social forestry. The *National Wasteland Development Board* was set. up to support, among others, voluntary organisations in their effort to "green the wastelands" of India.

More than three decades ago, an institution called *PADI (People's Action Development India)* was set up with a view to channelise resources from outside the country to rural development organisations; but, in its original form, it was not very active and effective. In 1986, the *Council for*

Advancement of Peoples' Action and Rural Technology (CAPART) was set up as an autonomous institution (incidentally registered under the Society Act) to finance voluntary organisations under various schemes and programmes. It is also interesting to note that CAPART could be used by voluntary organisations to organise and conscientise the poor.

Over the years, many voluntary organisations have utilised government funds and many continue to do so. A large number of them have depended totally on grants from the state. In many ways, the work of these voluntary organisations has been guided by the nature of the relationship between them and the state as a funder (one of a recipient to a donor). Clearly, in such a relationship, the recipient has weaker powers, control and autonomy with respect to the donor. Many consequences flow from this relationship. Firstly, most funding from the state is available for specific schemes and programmes, largely conceptualised and designed by the state itself. Voluntary organisations have to fit their proposals into those schemes and programmes, if they want those resources. Thus, voluntary organisations, over a period of time, become mere implementers of the ideas, concepts and programmes created by the state. This has a subsidiary effect because it defines a narrow space for voluntary organisations by providing funds for pre-designated schemes and programmes, mostly in the areas of welfare and development. Thus the work of voluntary organisations as a legitimate part of society is narrowly confined and defined. Another consequence of this has been increasing dependence of certain organisations on funds from the state. As such state mechanisms and institutions become increasingly bureaucratised and corrupt, and those voluntary organisations dependent on state funding have to face this increasing bureaucratisation and corruption within such state institutions and mechanisms. As a dependent recipient from the state donor, such voluntary organisations also experience the tension of attempting to work with bureaucratic and corrupt institutions in order to continue receiving the grants from the state. Various attempts have been made to modify these schemes, euphemistically called "grant-in-aid". The overall experience seems to indicate that availability of resources from the state for work of voluntary organisations is unique and useful, on the one hand, but has limiting, controlling and dependence-creating effects, on the other. In situations where such voluntary organisations have raised their voice against corruption and inefficiency of state agencies or officials, government funding has stopped midstream-what can be called the "crisis of the second installment". The overall impact of this has been a carrot-and-stick approach, under which funds are given to those who do not rock the boat or are willing to fit their work and activities within the programmes and schemes of the state and its bureaucrats. Funds have been stopped for those who tried to challenge the state, its strategies or programmes, its agents and representatives, through their own work. It seems that increasing bureaucratisation and control over mechanisms of funding has considerably undennined their autonomous functioning and, therefore, those voluntary organisations in a recipient-donor relationship with the state often find themselves in an uneasy situation.

Development Actor

The third dimension of this relationship has to be understood in the context of the state as a significant and dominant actor in the development arena. As a socialist welfare state defined through the constitution right from independence, various government schemes., departments and agencies have been started with a view to promote development. In virtually every area of development—health, education, provision of drinking water, sanitation, agriculture, rural development, forestry, environment, family planning-the government's own departments, programmes and schemes are most dominant and active. As a result, the space for voluntary organisations in the development arena has been increasingly shrinking. A consequence of this has been the use of development models and frameworks promoted by the state which are implemented through its own programmes. departments and schemes. Over the years, the state has established hegemony over such models of development and such frameworks. It, therefore, prefers that all other actors in the arena accept this. Voluntary organisations engaged in help, charity, welfare and narrow developmental activities have no difficulty in continuing to operate within the ambit of the state's hegemony role. However, others who question the policies and programmes of the. state, who promote new solutions and innovations which challenge the models of the state, which examine the consequences of following the state models in the form of continuing poverty and marginalisation and use their findings to influence public opinion, find that the state as the dominant development actor comes into conflict with them_ In such situations of conflict and confrontation; a variety of mechanisms are used by the state to sustain and perpetuate its hegemony over development models and frameworks. Regulatory mechanisms are one such weapon but perhaps more crucial and powerful is the use of the funding mechanism. By limiting availability of funds to its own programmes and schemes, by providing funds only to certain types of voluntary organisations, by creating fund-related dependence on itself among large sections of voluntary organisations, the state maintains its hegemony. Repression, intimidation, harassment, rejection and delegitimisation of those who question this hegemony of the state as a development actor is a natural consequence very frequently encountered by 'offending' bodies.

Another serious consequence of this hegemony has been that the State has been trying to monopolise all resources, internal and external. Thus all bilateral funds from countries of the North, all funds from the multilateral institutions of the UN system must be approved, controlled and regulated and primarily used by the state and its agents in the promotion of state organised or approved development activities. In fact, there is a continuous effort within this framework to establish the supreme role of the state as a development actor and appropriate to itself all resources, internal as well as external. Several moves in recent years have been made by the state and its agents to even capture all external funds coming from non-government sources from the North. Under the guise of regulating their disbursal to "well-meaning" voluntary organisations, the combination of the state as a funder and the state as a development actor has proved to be so powerful in the Indian context that many voluntary organisations find themselves dependent and incapacitated to challenge the frameworks and models of development promoted by the state and thus the hegemony of the state continues.

Relationships

As a consequence of the development roles assumed by the state during the past five decades, there have been some significant consequences for the structure and quality of relationships that have enterged between voluntary action and the state in India.

Dependency

The most common, the predominant form of relationship between governments, central and state, and voluntary organisations is that of dependent-client. This dependency/ clientism arises in situations where voluntary organisations are either implementing development programmes prepared by the state and its agencies, or receiving funds from the state-, or both. It is a dependency of ideas, money, resources.

An analysis of the experience in many other countries of the South seems to indicate that funding by the government is largely available only for the development programmes and strategies prepared by the government itself. This dependency/clientism was most common and widespread among those voluntary organisations which are providing social services or are engaged in welfare work. These are also the ones which are the largest recipients of government funding.

Adversarial

A second type of relationship between a voluntary organisation and government could be characterised as *adversarial,* where the two are perpetually locked in conflicts. This is common among voluntary organisations which challenge the policies of the state, its development frameworks and paradigms. The same is true of voluntary organisations which directly support people's organisations and social movements. It is a relationship in which the government perceives voluntary organisations as opponents per se raising issues and concerns and operating in ways and adopting means which challenge the policies of the government its programmes and strategies, the assumptions underlying its frameworks and models, and the practices of its representatives and agents. In situations in which government officials were identified as segments of the vested interests exploiting, marginalising and harassing the poor, the action of voluntary organisations obviously contributes towards the empowerinent of the poor vis-a-vis their oppressors. Building peoples' organisations, strengthening social movements and challenging vested interests is not always welcomed by higher government authorities, rather it is perceived as an attack on the officers of the government, its structures and apparatus. In other situations, where the voluntary organisations are working to check authoritarianism, to promote participatory democracy, to win for the people a greater access to information and a greater voice in the planning and control by the people of the development process, their work is seen as hostile to the very structures and the styles of functioning of the government and its departments-a questioning of the bureaucratic, unilateral, secretive and centralised style of functioning. In many specific situations, the actions of voluntary organisations arise out of the mis-governance and malfunctioning of the government agencies and programmes.Thus we have a built-in conflict of interest whenever the government functioning and/or political leaders are criticised and challenged.

Co-operation

In the third type of relationship, the emphasis is on a healthy co-operation between voluntary organisations and the goverinient authorities and machinery; differences are discussed and understood by the parties: common areas of action on policy and programine aspects are identified in which voluntary organisations and government can work together. Issues of health, education, micro-finance, environment, drinking water, housing etc. are common areas for such co-operation. Issues of macro-economic policy, natural resource management, rights over funds, human rights, land reforms etc. are perpetually contested arenas in the Indian context. In recent years, voluntary organisations and government have co-operated at the national level to deal with the positions and arguments of the countries of the north concerning WTO, structural adjustment policies urged by the World Bank/IMF, and bio-diversity treaties.

Emerging Ambiguities

In view of this range of roles, functions and relationships, several dilemmas and tensions arise in the interaction between voluntary organisations and the state. These cannot be wished away; they cannot be resolved on a 'once and for all' basis; their recurrence is inevitable, as would be the case in any active relationship. Voluntary organisations have to find ways to work through them in specific situations.

Vuluntarism vs Privatisation

One growing trend in recent years is the promotion of voluntary organisations under the guise of promoting privatisation of social services for the amelioration of conditions of the poor in the rural hinterlands and urban slums. The "structure adjustment policies" of the World Bank/IMF are encouraging many governments to withdraw from provision of social services in health, education, drinking water, etc. The private sector is encouraged to play the role of service provision as well as generation of income for the poor and the deprived. It is within this context that a question haunts one: Is not increased support for voluntary service organisations from multilateral, international and governmental sources likely to push them, the service organisations, into supporting the trend towards privatisation of services? It is important to ensue that voluntary organisations play only a supportive role and do not themselves become the providers, taking on the responsibilities of the state in this behalf. Voluntary organisations must, of course, provide necessary services in critical situations, when it in crucial that they do so, but they must guard against displacing the official delivery mechanisms altogether thereby absolving the state of its responsibility of performing its moral and constitutional duty in this regard. Many voluntary organisations find themselves increasingly playing the role of provider of basic services for the poor. This is particularly so in the case of organisations working in tribal and dalit communities, for which the government has failed in its duty to provide basic education and primary health care. A judicious choice has to be made and delicate balances have to be maintained when addressing the problems of such situations.

Co-operation vs Sub-contracting

Increasingly, governments are calling upon voluntary organisations in many countries of the South to get involved in the promotion of development programmes, largely those designed by the State itself. Even where some of these programmes appear to be based on voluntary-organisation recommended development principles and assumptions, many voluntary organisations are finding that their co-operation with the State; in a large measure, becomes undertaking a subcontract for fulfilling of development targets and completion of programmes. The nature of the relationship becomes one of the contractor acrd the sub-contractor, where the voluntary organisations receive a certain payment for fulfilling certain targets prescribed by the state within a given development framework. It is, therefore, important to examine. each specific case of co-operation and the extent to which the terms of that co-operation are reducing the role of voluntary organisations to mere commercial implementers of a programme and achievers of targets for and on behalf of they government. This has been particularly so in health and family welfare programmes throughout the world and is increasingly being seen in relation to literacy and education.

Yet, in many situations in India, voluntary organisations are nevertheless willing to take part in government development programmes. An important consideration is that taking over implementation of a programme ensures that resources available for that programme are utilised effectively and that its fruit reach the intended berlefieianes. By gaining access to such programmes, voluntary organisations also get opportunities to influence the nature of the programmes themselves.

Disagreement vs Opposition

The work of voluntary organisations throws up experiences, ideas and perspectives which are based on realities in micro settings at the grassroots level. This evokes diverse opinions, approaches and analyses, many a times in opposition to the perspectives and analyses of the government, its officials and agencies. This sort of disagreement also occurs between voluntary organisations and political parties as the analyses and perspectives of the two often differ on many issues and occasions. These disagreements should not be seen as political opposition in a narrow sense of the term. Disagreement is not necessarily unhealthy in such situations. Development and social transformation are complex phenomena and no simple or single solution is available for all of the problems they throw up in any given setting. Therefore, the availability of a multiplicity of views, experiences and analyses can only be healthy in seeking to resolve some of these developmental knots.

However, differences and disagreements are generally viewed as deliberate antagonism and opposition by governments, its officials and agencies, parties and their politbureaus. This attitude tends to provoke responses from the governments and political parties that tend to discourage the expression of differences and delegitimise those engaged in such expression. It is important to distinguish between differences and disagreements on the one hand, and deliberate opposition, on the other.

This is the most important issue affecting the state-voluntary agency relationship, the issue of co-existence with mutual respect, dignity and autonomy. The state, its agencies and officials are relatively much more powerful in relation to individual voluntary organisations and groups of voluntary organisations in many countries of the South. This is certainly the case in India. They are much more resourceful, much better informed and much better equipped to deal with resourceless, mostly uninformed and ill-equipped voluntary organisations. Yet, on many occasions, the relationship demands co-operation and co-existence. The challenge is, how can this co-operation occur without undermining the autonomy and independence of the voluntary organisations. The dilemma is that the latter require resources and capacities, which the state and its agencies have, can offer and should offer. How can the provision of resources and capacities from the state and its agencies to the voluntary- organisations ht dene in a manner that does not undermine the autonomy and independence of the latter, but, in fact, contributes towards strengthening them?

Questioning vs Weakening

A major role of voluntary organisations has been to critique and question the policies, programmes and strategies of the government. This critique has been raised through direct lobbying and personal advocacy, through publications, debates and discourses, workshops, seminars and training programmes, through the mobilisation and empowerrnent of the people themselves, through the networks and federations etc: This is necessary, healthy and crucial.

Yet in situations where the state is withering away, or the state is weakening as a consequence of international forces, continued and indiscriminate questioning may further support the forces that weaken or strangulate the state. This has become particularly relevant in the context of the international scenario that has been adopted in recent years. Voluntary organisations may occasionally co-operate with the state to challenge and oppose more powerful international forces affecting the country, the government- and the people. This has often been the case in India. However the Indian government has resisted questioning by voluntary organisations in international fora. Whenever voluntary organisations have challenged the position of the

Government of India in UN conferences and commissions (like at Beijing, Copenhagen, Vienna, Cairo and Istanbul), government officials and political leaders have criticised such voluntary organisations. A recent. case in point is the issue of caste (dailts) in the Durban Conference on Xenophobia.

Thus, support to voluntary organisations by government policies and funds has been an important part of the growth and vibrancy of voluntary organisations in India. Voluntary organisations have had the capacity and freedom to question and challenge the government. The principle of peaceful coexistence with dignity despite disagreements needs to be the operating credo of this relationship.

5

National Development and Voluntary Sector

The dimensions of the problems in India, like the country itself, are mind boggling. The situation becomes all the more critical for a nation caught-up between the growth, buoyancy and the rising expectations on the one hand, and the relative deprivation of the majority, wide spread despondency on the other. The span of 55 years of our independence has proved most inadequate for us in tackling the problems of India i.e. fulfilling, the basic needs of food, shelter, clothing and basic amenities of life; quality growth in education, health and other such human resource related infrastructure. In absolute numbers poverty has compounded manifolds, a large section of our population, over 65 to 70% still below or at bare subsistence level, whatever be the measurement or considerations to ascertain the 260 million people being below the poverty line in the last count. For them, each day being a fresh struggle for existence, the enormous and unparalleled human potential of India mostly remains untapped. The government 'for the people, by the people and of the people' has not really lived up to their expectations. The gap between 'haves' and 'have-nots' has been widening exponentially, the have-nots numerically increasing in geometrical proportions. In the wake of the much publicized and widely acclaimed globalization, privatization and liberalization, there is a strong, a well orchestrated demand for the Government to withdraw even from some of the constitutional obligations of a welfare state. The much talked about Corporate (Business) social responsibilities is yet to take any real shape in the larger context of the voluntary sector in India. Consequently, the NGOs, the most commonly accepted expressions for the voluntary sector, have no option but to grow and come to the forefront to shoulder direct responsibilities and play their historic role.

Taking of development, it has not been commensurate with the aspirations, expectations and, more pertinently, with the planned allocations and the expenditure. So much so that some problems inflicting the country at the time of independence persists in a more compounded manner, thanks to our ever increasing population. Besides our recent achievements in IT and some other sectors of growth directly or indirectly touching upon 10-20% of our population, ironically, we seem to occupy the global centre stage in population, but given the present status of our human development in terms of the basic necessities of life, we do not really cover ourselves with glory. With over 1020 million people inhabiting the country, the issues relating to illiteracy, out-of-school-children, child labour, infant and child mortality, physically and mentally challenged population, the growing number of uncared elders, our problems are ever exceeding our resources. In case the diminishing employment opportunities are any pointer, we are far from converting our population into really useful human resources for the national development.

The allocations, schemes, policies and programmes for women, children, elders, disabled, socially defenseless, and in the crucial sectors of health and education, have though been rising and multiplying in the anual and 5 years plans, their tangible impact is yet to be seen in raising why plethora of legislations meant to safeguard the interests of the weak and vulnerable have, by and large, remained unsuccessful in fulfilling their cherished objectives. Status of women and children causes particular concern. Article 45, for example, meant to ensure compulsory education upto 14 years of age could not achieve the desired results, and now the 93rd amendment to the Constitution casting a legal obligation, less upon the state and more on the incapable or impoverished families and the undefined Community, is to be tested on the ground.

A close look at the crucial sectors of social development gives on idea about the mammoth task in hand. The problems relating to poverty and deprivation, hunger, homelessness and the absence of the basic life sustaining conditions, are most real. We have the largest number of people affected by poverty and destitution in the world. Our own estimation indicate over 72 million families being in situation of absolute poverty and millions dying every year due to hunger, malnutrition and ill health. Nearly 13 million 'houseless households' found in census-2001 multiplied by 5 each, meaning 6.5 crores homeless people happened to be in the country[1]. With nearly 30% of the population now inhabiting in the last enumerated 5161 urban centers in the country, there were 100 million people among them living in urban slums without or with little access to water, sanitation, health care and with sparse education facilities for the neglected, street and working children. Such unhappy development profiles are further crossed by numerous situations of socio-economic conflicts and crisis in myriad forms that pose major challenge to the governance.

In the given situation, there is a need to ascertain the role of voluntary sector which stands transfixed somewhere between an insensitive civil society, a doubly insensitive Govt. machinery and socially indifferent political leadership right from the levels of Panchayati Raj institutions and Municipal Bodies to the states and national leadership.

1 Census of India 2001

Although, many in the voluntary sector and even outside, prefer to be called Voluntary Action Group (VOLAGS) or voluntary organization etc, the most common term used even now happens to be Non-Governmental Organizations. The emergence of such NGOs representing the most visible participation of the civil society on common issues of public concern is a global phenomenon. However, the significance of such non-governmental efforts to achieve the same goals as that of a welfare State through community or non-governmental efforts, finds a new meaning in the developing countries of South-East Asia and Africa. The NGOs are in existence in American and European countries as well, but in these individualistic and the capitalistic societies, the private endeavours to achieve similar goals are far more pervasive and institutionalized for altruistic and personal gains. The voluntary organizations in these countries serve a limited purpose, particularly to look after the disadvantaged and disabled sections of society, more in the nature of specialized activities where the government does not take major responsibilities and the business and the profit making organizations operate to merely express the social concerns. Contray to them, in the developing countries, the NGOs or the voluntary organizations are often seen as the main driving force in the process of socio-economic mobilization and change. For instance, in Bangladesh, the powerful NGOs like Gramin Bank and Bangladesh Rural Advancement Committee (BRAC) have almost substituted the Govt. in the areas of women's empowerment and micro-credit and primary education respectively, reaching out to several millions.

In the changing times, in India as well, the NGOs are slated, though not yet substantially poised to play the pivotal role in the field of education and child development. They have emerged as an important feature on the Indian social landscape and, for appropriate reasons, the 21st century is being described as the decade of NGOs. Whereas, the growth of voluntary sector is becoming pronounced worldwide, in India it attains far more significance on account of the need for massive participation of the people. With the State parcelling out a number of its responsibilities to the voluntary sector, and many non-profit organizations undertaking entrepreneurial activities to subsidize their charitable operations, the line between the various sectors of activities, like the State voluntary groups and the corporates, is getting blurred. What then will be the distinctive contribution of the voluntary sector, and where lies its comparative advantage?

During its long journey, volunteerism as the precursor and the constant driving force behind the voluntary efforts has changd not only in form but also in spirit. In the past, religion, western liberal and humanist thought, leftist ideologies, and Gandhian philosophy served as the inspiration for volunteerism. Those drawn to voluntary action believed in simple, almost austere, living and total commitment, but this is not necessarily so now. Today, the dominant motive may be said to be enlightened self-interest. Unless poverty and inequalities are reduced, violence and discrimination controlled, and the environment protected, the future for everyone will be blank. The voluntary efforts now witness a paradigm shift to meet up these high expectations and to tackle the issues of common concern, some relating to the very survival of mankind. Still, the demands being made from the voluntary sector is somewhat unrealistic, indeed unreasonable. The volunteers or social workers, in the common parlance, are supposed to perform without being paid and act mostly in the spirit of charity. We have to understand that volunteers are not a class of people who are supposed to be driven by emotions nd sense of social service alone, as if they have no needs of day-to-day existence, livelihood or any demands towards themselves and their families. Over the years, fortunately, when the activists and managers in the voluntary sector are attempting to institutionalize the efforts, their attempts are now being at least recognized as a necessary complement, even an alternative to the governmental efforts. In the policies and programmes of the government, particularly in the social sector, in most of the schemes being implemented by the national and the State Governments, there is at least ritualistic mention of voluntary efforts. It is besides the point that the voluntary efforts are still not being taken to be a serious alternative except in case of some known NGOs who have created capacities that can't be overlooked and acclaimed models.

From our point of view, the volunteerism is now synonymous with multiple variety of voluntary efforts, described as volunteers, social workers, NGOs, voluntary organizations, voluntary action groups, or community based organizations. Besides these the numerous Trusts, Foundations, Cooperatives, Trade Unions, societies are also playing a significant role. In fact, considering the status of the Panchayati Raj institutions despite the 73rd Amendment to the Constitution and other grass-root democratic organizations, like other local self-governments, even they may also fall somewhere between the Govt. and the voluntary sector. Although, such democratic institutions are constitutionally supposed to be apolitical, in practice and due to the electoral process involved, they have become highly politicized. They have to carry the conviction of voluntary sector for a fair democratic participation at the grass-root level touching upon all aspects of the people's live of the 70% of the Indians. When we discuss about the volunteerism and the role of this sector in tackling the national issues, such as, universal education, health & family planning and poverty alleviation, we cannot permit the grass-root democratic institutions to abdicate their primary responsibility.

Needless to mention that the voluntary efforts, albeit, in a more organized and institutionalized manner having the sanction and support of the Govt. and the larger society, holds the key to the basic transformation of the country. It is also being realized that the massive programmes like, Sarva Shiksha Abhiyan (Education For All) or the Universal Education still remains a far cry with. about 70-80 million out-of-school children, dropouts in the absence of the entire being is given the shape of a nationwide movement. Since all previous efforts, like National Literacy (Mission) Programme could not truly take off in a mission mode, as pronounced; the latest and the most ambitious, Sarv Shiksha Abhiyan also may not succeed without a nation-wide voluntary participation. Out of nearly 400 million children who are found below 18 years of age in the sizeable numbers being out-of-school system. Half of them being dropouts on account of either due to adverse socio-economic conditions or for the reason that the formal. school system in most of the villages, towns, even in bigger cries like Delhi, are not able to create any interest or occupational or entrepreneurships opportunities leading to decent placements in life. As a result, there appears to be a major divide in the society in the name of education and, ultimately, a miniscule of the population, a very small segment, receives meaningful education. One basic reason for this gap between what is needed and what is available in the name of service delivery, appears to be the lack of participation by the civil society and the absence of options from the informed choices. It is only with the support and participation of the voluntary sector that the national policies can be correctly formulated and appropriate infrastructure, curricula and systems can be created to deliver the requisite services to the masses.

Similarly is the situation with all other major programmes of the government in the social sector projects and schemes, which are now being taken to the local self government. What is missing at the cutting edge level is meaningful partnership between the government, local self functionaries and most importantly people's participation that is possible only through associating and organizing the voluntary efforts.

Voluntary Sector in India

In pre-independent India, the voluntary sector was perceived as a charity and, at times, as a vehicle to promote national integration and independence movement. During post independence period, the voluntary sector has emerged as a new force contributing to social development while also plugging gaps in the Government run programs. Flexibility and informal systems of functioning has brought VOs closer to the beneficiaries allowing them to take speedier and well targeted action, invariably at a lower cost. VOs have brought into focus issues like health, education, rural and urban development, environment protection, women and child welfare and they have become an inalienable part of the contemporary development scene. No doubt, they have carved out a definitive place for themselves, as being reported, but they have yet to emerge as a viable alternative. The total number in the country officially stands nearly 2 million, most of them happen to be very small in size and impact, rural-based, and majority unregistered.

Unfortunately, the term 'voluntary sector', same as the other much-maligned expressions like bureaucracy and the government, has acquired somewhat dubious connotation. People, even those well placed in the government and in other responsible positions talk about the voluntary sector as being 'rackets' or agencies that try to corner and misuse the government and nongovernmental funds. The voluntary sector's credibility is at a low level during a period of our times when they should be poised to play a historic role in the social development. This is unfortunate because it is the sector of our organized civil society that can assist the nation liberate from the morass of utter hopelessness, poverty and

---

Census of India 2001

the sub-human existence in which 60-70% of the Indians are still living.

The role of the voluntary sector also needs to be understood in the context of our sovereign, democratic, republic which under the Constitution, social legislations and plethora of policy and international documents is expected to create an egalitarian, healthy, happy and a just society. In the given context, the role of the voluntary sector is crucial and needs to be defined in the overall scenario, particularly with reference to the government which operates like a giant, striding over all sectors of our activities. Its interventions must not remain limited to a supplementary role or only in being opposition to the government. Social and economic development programmes and activities of the national and provincial government that aimed at empowerment have reduced the ordinary people into 'beneficiaries'

In fact, the government can play a very important role in terms of facilitating the VOs throughout the country ensuring their even growth. Now, the efforts towards the enhancement of the voluntary sector need to be strengthened and synergized. This sector is an asset because being community-based, it is capable of delivering inexpensive' services at the level and alongwith the people it is supposed to serve at a lesser cost. More significantly, the VOs are able to develop innovative projects based on the locally felt-needs and the available resources as against the governmental stereotypes. The present situations significantly highlight the importance of the GO-VO interface which may act as focal points from where integrated and holistic view could be taken on the voluntary sector.

The participation of VOs in sustainable social development who may act as partners in the process of socio-economic changes and in the nation-building is critical. Expansion of activities and growth of macro-level leadership in the voluntary sector is possible through the networks of local leadership within the sector. There is a need to enhance the capacity, of the commurity-based VOs, SHGs and women's groups through the mobilization of the existing resources, which is possible only through the partnerships in government and, private sectors which may subsume corporate sector, industrial houses, charitable trusts set-up by NRls, individual donors and business houses even the international support.

Hence, there is a need to focus on the replicable models of the voluntary sector led development and deliver services that do not depend on the governmental intervention alone for its growth. The voluntary sector or VOs can indeed play a substantial role in the welfare and development of children, women, and capacity-building of others in the same field. Creating a federating body of VOs at the state and district levels could further facilitate the work of the voluntary sector. One visualizes a triangular partnership between the government, business entit'es, both as individuals and organizations -who were called the Trustees for People's wealth by Mahatma Gandhi, and the voluntary organisations at all levels concentrated upon the areas of real and urgent socio-economic needs, particularly education, child protection and health in order to bring about real changes.

There are also numerous public spirited individuals, both in India and abroad, who volunteer for the social cause while making their bits of contributions towards the larger goal of social development. In the present scenario, we really need to acknowledge their contributions and motivate them not only to continue their work but also to set them as role models for many others who have the spirit but they need some support and direction. The immense contributions made by the social workers, both in India and abroad, also needs to be acknowledged.

One needs to understand that none of these political and administrative systems can truly ensure any effective grass-root participation unless carried out as a people's movement.

Perceived in the backdrop of the national realities, as they confront us, the voluntary sector must ultimately wake up to its potentials and play the crucial role which joining hands with the grassroots democratic institutions and the government at all levels to create a truly participative and inclusive governance.

Volume and Scale of the Voluntary Sector

In the absence of any centralized databank or nationally coordinated system of information on the voluntary sector today, it is impossible to provide accurate and precise estimates of the scale and size of the voluntary sector. However, there are an estimated 2 million voluntary initiatives and organizations in the country which include a wide diversity of local youth clubs. Mahilla Mandals, private schools, hospitals, even some government constituted voluntary organizations like CAPART, Jan Shikshan Sansthan, etc. How many of these smaller organizations are still alive and functional is hard to estimate. Estimating the scale of resources being used by the voluntary sector is even more difficult. Nearly 25000 organizations are reportedly now registered under FCRA and they receive nearly Rs. 4000 crores in the year 1999-2000[1]. Different Ministris and Departments of the national and state governments have formulated a vast number of schemes[2]. We may hazard a guess that nearly the same amount, as the foreign contribution, comes from the government departments and agencies, including large development projects funded by bilateral and multilateral agencies. In addition, India has had a long tradition of volunteering and giving and thus contributions from ordinary people and community continue to be received by the voluntary sector.

1 Ministry of Home Affairs, Government of India.

2 Report of the Steering Committee on Voluntary Sector for the 10th Five Year Plan January, 2002

The preliminary findings of PRIA present a detailed and interesting account of the volume and scale of the VOs operating in India. The identity of the VOs in India remains largely invisible, despite that the sector in India is widespread, its scale is huge and significant on several accounts, employment, revenue and the types of activities. And this scale of VOs demands serious attention and strong support from policy-makers, government officials and political leders. More than half the VOs in the country are based in rural areas, while even those based in urban area mostly serve the rural communities. The Indian NPOs are essentially small and nearly three-fourth of all VOs are reported to have only volunteers or at the most one or two paid staff. Only one in 12 VOs employs more then 10 paid staff. Nation wide nearly 20 million persons work on a paid or volunteer basis in VOs out of which only 27 lakh (2.7 million) are full-time equivlent paid employees. The findings outlined that the VOs were mainly engaged in five dominant activities, Sports/Culture, Religious (engaged in social development), Community / social service, Educational and Health.

The research further estimated to show that the total receipts by VOs for 1999-2000 were Rs 17,922 crores, which were primarily generated though loans, grants, donations or were self generated. More than half of all receipts of VOs in India are self-generated through fees or charges for services, etc. 75 million households (40.7%) gave for charitable causes. A percentage as high as 68% of all givers (2/3rd) were rural based. 2/5th of all givers were poor households with an annual income below Rs. 25,000.

The GO-VO Interface

The relation between the State (or the Government) and the NGOs in India has been mostly viewed in somewhat myopic perspective, particularly social action groups emphasizing rights based approach, who often find themselves in situations of conflict while giving voice to or organizing the poor nd the deprived. In this context, one of the classifications done as Corporate NGOs, Development Oriented NGOs and NGOs professing Development with Social Justice, deserves a mention. Together, or distinguished from the social action groups, the community development voluntary organizations have significant role to play, whether in prtnership with the Government or alone with the grass-root democratic institutions with corporate sector, through international or national funding, through institutions, NRIs or othrwise, No doubt, the voluntary organizations have special role to play in advocating, networking and articulating the struggle from the local to the global levels, they have to mobilize the people and work towards for justice, to fulfill socio-economic, legal and potential rights which are intertwined with the day to day realities of life and individual needs. However, the direct role of voluntary organization to tackle the multiple and gigantic problems besetting us perhaps attains special significance.

A look of the government as the largest service delivery sector reflects disquieting gaps, even between what the government plans to spend and the benefits society gains out of it. This can be addressed in strategic manner by roping in various segments of population to achieve common national mission. In the same context, it is felt that the success of any government is of the democratic institutions, entirely rests on the people's participation. Our functional democracy, like most other indirect democratic systems end up becoming electoral representative institutions with major consideration in the reality of power politics. The government, of its policy formulation level, functions through the Parliament, State Assemblies and other such bodies, and at the execution level, if is the bureaucracy, which runs the system in India the Nehruvion vision, of three-tier democratic participation, including the PRIs has not yet taken shape in true even the proper constitutional sense.

For argument s sake, even if the PR's and the munlcipal bodies come to occupy their rightful positions in terms of the 73rd or 74th Constitutional amendments(1993), the System essentially rernains political power-centric. Their role the process of Socio-economic transformation and in imparting justice legal or other wise, is yet to find a form. One needs to understand that none of these political arid administrative swems car truly ensure the real gross-roof participation unless carried out as a people's movement. From the national realities, as they confront us, it is difficult to identify such a leadership or a cadre of workers which is going to create movement of the requi site dimension. The only sector which must ultimately wake up to its real potentials and play its role would be the Voluntary sector joining hands with the grass-root democratic institutions and the government at all levels to create truly participative and inclusive governance. Hence, at this point of time, the role of the VOs needs to be strengthened and synergized.

Innovations in the Field of VO

Yet another implication of the alcove mentioned modes collaborations is to identity and agree on areas for joint action oy NGOs and government. We feel that issues of poverty, education, health and population ore some of the key-areas. May it be noted that partnership means joint action at ail the levels of policy and programme planning and implementation. This does no preclude independent action on the part of either government or NGOs.

Voluntary organisations have been experimenting with new ways of promoting more sustainable, people-centred development. Through flexible, at times even risk-taking experimentation, they have been able to develop methods, models and equipments that have been widely adopted by the state and national governments as well as the international agencies. Many national development progrmme of —

Government of India, based on such inovations promoted by voluntary organisations, include areas lik non-formal education, innovative methods of literary, primary healthcare, blogas, community-forestry; and in recent years, self-help groups, micro-credit and income generation programmes.

In undertaking such projects, voluntary organizations require flexible resources and a process-oriented approach not bogged down by bureaucratic rules and procedures. Scalling-up such innovations by voluntary organisations also requires an understanding of the "software", natue of this work without insising on short-term target-orientation.

Voluntary Sector: The Alternative Path of Social Development in India

In India, once we attempt get into the dimension of the problems that we face, we realize their distributing mammoth proportions, to the extent that the planners, policy makers, national and international resource providers almost throw up their hands in hopelessness. The dynamics of Indian people, divided in endless number of ways, regions to caste and communities ancient, medieval to modern, co-existing, some sections of the population keeping pace with the latest trends in the global economy further multiply and compound the issues involved.

In our experience, the first and the central challenge is to redefine our understanding of the various sectors of activities in our national life, including the voluntary sector. A monolithic approach towards the voluntary sector does not carve out a positive role for them although they seem to complement the efforts of the state governmental as an alternative system of governance. Despite the limited resources and the shift in the government's policy that

1 (GARAIN (1994), Development Hegemony, NGOs and the Development in India. Sangeeta Kamat)

further prepares to andicate part of the welfare activities, the complementary and the alternative function of the voluntary sector is yet to be recognized. This situation creates a major yawning gap between what is being done in the social sector and what needs to be done.

As far as the corporate sector is concerned, it has made some contributions for the societal development but all its efforts are through the individual institutions. In terms of the quantum of support being provided by the corporate world under the much talked about corporate social responsibility in India, it appears quite small, couple of thousand and crores rupees. Hence, emerges the role *of* the third, the most important sector of the voluntary organizations to fill the gap. So far this sector has also not really addressed the core areas. Its outreach is very small, almost insignificant compared to the government sector. For instance an organised voluntary efforts in rural development is yet to take shape. The voluntary efforts in rural development in terms of geographical coverage is insignificnt as compared to the needs of the country. As per some estimates only 3 to 4 percent of the 0.75 million villages in the country are covered by voluntary action'. This sector cannot be just viewed as 'a charitable work' but is as a major partner in the development process.

If we talk of participatory governance, it can be understood in three forms, namely, the electoral government, the Panchayati Raj Institutions (PRIs) and the VOs. Hence, what is required is a partnership between the three, the unique component of the voluntary sector being the 'bottom up' approach and not 'top to bottom' approach of the government. This implies that the voluntary sector necessarily involves participation from the grass root levels.

Now, when we look at the VOs from the point of view of the functional democracy then we actually realize that they are as much democratic institutions as the PRIs since organizations, even they emerge from the people's needs and their efforts are for the people. The innovations, empowerment, research and advocacy by the VOs are also unique having distinct features as those NGOs themselves. The need thus emerges enable this most important sector of national activity, the VOs to grow so that this get evenly distributed throughout the country and.take-up larger responsibilities in partnership with the LSGs/PRIs and the government.

The VOs are playing an important role in providing and shaping an alternative path of development on the basis of the felt-needs of the community and by involving a great deal of community participation. In the voluntary sector there is urgent requirement of capacity-building of the smaller voluntary organisations through the reputed and diversified organizations. This would also creates enhance networking amongst the voluntary sector working in the same field. The leaders, opinion makers and the resource providers have to appreciate and accept the crucial role to be played by the voluntary sector in the task of national development. The role of the government increasingly being reduced to defense, law and orders, financial controls and such other activities of the State, the role of corporate-industrial-commercial sector being limited to the market driven activities, some of the real task of social development, inevitably, falls upon the voluntary sector. With the changing times and perception in the Indian socio-economic scenario, there appears to be major void to be filled by the combination of grassroots democratic institutions and voluntary organisations.

PRAYAS (Delhi Based Organisation)

In a situation of intensely felt need from a major fire in a slum cluster of Delhi which devastated 5000 houses leaving

---

1 VANI, Voluntarism and Government. 2 001

thousands of children homeless, from 25 children to this day, Prayas has traveled a long way. Now, it accesses nearly 50,000 street children and their proximate communities in the states of Delhi, Gujarat and Bihar. It has been an extremely arduous journey. Today, with nearly 62 centres of alternative education, 16 centres of excellent vocational training, well organized health services catering to the needs of 50,000 street and slum children alone in Delhi running several Children's Homes for the homeless, and an excellent Child Helpline programme, the organisation has become the focal point of change and development in the slums of Delhi, villages of Gujarat and state level programme for rehabilitation of abandoned children in Bihar.

Prayas, 'a modest effort' as the name suggests, this NGO has become a vehicle and a medium of change in the lives of thousands of families and communities in the areas of real needs, always responding to its infringing faith that the needs and the rights of children are synonymous. Having the powerful infrastructure including some most vibrant structures in these three States, this organisation is today prepared for a significant role in the process of social development and social change wherever it operates. It impacts directly on the lives of thousands of slum and village communities with multiple programmes of education, health care, self help, microcredit activities and vocational training, programmes, helpline services through its apex body, Prayas Institute of Juvenile Justice, having research and documentation, information, education and communication, training and resources units, Prayas is acting in close partnership with the government and major voluntary networks at the local, national and international levels.

The organisation visualizes its role in the larger scheme of the voluntary vis-a-vis social development sector in India. Fortunately, this NGO has developed some excellent linkages abroad both, in terms of international organisations, namely, NORAD, USAID, Aus-AID, CIDA, besides a number of nongovernmental organisations and individuals abroad. In USA, it operates in partnership with Children's Hope Inc. and a chapter of the organisation opening soon with the support group of highly committed Indian in the country. In Germany, for years now, Prayas is operating a chapter with the help of some dedicated voluntary organisations working with local schools on the issue of environment. We recently participated in a major global consciousness meeting organized by the Club of Budapest at Frankfurt. In U.K., Prayas has found hundreds of committed supporters who have recently, decided to open chapters within and outside the country.

'We, at Prayas, visualize ourselves as partners in a National and Global campaign to restore childhood to millions of children deprived of their basic needs. We wish to give them back their childhood in terms of care, protection and opportunities for participation and development.'

The Government democratic institutions voluntary sector interface may act as the focal point from where an integrated and holistic view of the voluntary sector could be taken. The voluntary, community-based development oriented organizations happen to be closer to the poor and the disadvantaged sections of the society. Essentially expected to be the products of the felt-need situations, the voluntary organizations have a much greater potential for innovations. As against the governmental stereotypes, rule-bound status quoits, the VOs are mostly unusual, flexible and prepared to change the times. Most of the well meaning voluntary organizations naturally respond to the development needs, work in multi-sectorol framework that also attempt to coordinate with the government having convergence with other motivated, local bodies and civil society organization and groups. The voluntary initiatives, whether in the form of community-based or social action organizations, they are much better placed to stimulate and mobilize community based support, enroll and utilize volunteers, and not only catalyze but also create social cohesion.

Volunteerism and NGOs

NGO embrace a bewildering group of organizations varying in terms of innumerable parameters. No standard definition can include all organizations under the omnibus caption - 'NGO'. In the common parlance, volunteerism and NGOs may be talked about as being two facets of a. similar kind of activities - the first being in the nature of a spirit and the second being organizational. Volunteerism is considered to be a doctrine in which a free will of an individual to act is a dominant factor. A volunteer is a person who offers services spontaneously without any extra incentives. His work is conscious, automatic and instinctively different from such a desire translated into some planned goal oriented activity. A voluntary organization may also be considered to be a conglomeration of volunteers joining hands with shared values of common concern for specific goals and the raison de'tre of such an organization is based on interests and objectives of a group constituting the organization.

Although, many in the voluntary sector and even outside, prefer to called voluntary Action Group (VOLAGS) or voluntary organization etc, the most common term even now happens to be non-governmental organisations. The emergence of such NGOs as presenting the participation of the civil society on common issues of concern is a global phenomenon.

However, the significance of such non-governmental efforts to achieve the same goals as that of a welfare State through community or non-governmental efforts, finds a new meaning in the developing countries of South-East Asia and Africa. Non-governmental organization or NGO had emerged as an important feature of the Indian social landscape, and the 21St century may be described as the age of the NGOs.

This development is not specific or limited to countries like India the NGOs are in existence in American and European countries as well. But the individualistic and the capitalistic societies, the private endeavours to achieve the similar goals are far more pervasive and institutionalized for both altruistic and personal reasons. The voluntary organisations in this sector serve the limited purpose, particularly to look after the disadvantaged and disabled sections of society, more in the nature of specialized activities where the government does not take many responsibilities and when the business and the profit making organisations operate more to express these social concerns. However, in the developing countries, the NGOs or the voluntary organizations are often seen as one of the main driving forces in the process of socio-economic mobilization and change. For instance, in Bangladesh, the massive NGOs like Gramin Bank and Bangladesh Rural Advancement Committee (BRAC) have almost taken the position of the Govt. in the areas of women empowerment and microcredit and primary education, respectively, reaching out to several millions.

The growth of the voluntary sector worldwide will surely rank among the outstanding developments of the present millennium. in India, it has an almost 100-year history of development. Ahead lies this new millennium which is likely to see a major redrawing of the boundaries as well as merging and complementary roles between the state, the market and civil society. It is important, therefore, to take stock of where the sector stands today and to also ascertain where it is heading in the future.

After five decades of educational programmes neither illiteracy nor the associated problems of social exclusion and gender discrimination have disappeared. Similar situations obtain in several other fields like health, sanitation and sub-standard living conditions, particularly in the context of children, women, disabled and the eiders people are increasingly becoming distrustful of the ability of public institutions and government agencies to deliver good governance. While the trend for greater privatization will help promote voluntary initiative, it is also likely to create a demand for a better balance between growth and quality education and health care. On the positive side, today we appear to be in a developmental stage, volunteerism will again become important aspect for social change that also led to social justice.

In some of these countries, the NGOs are seen as the main driving force in the social change and mobilization. NGOs are now pivotal in the field of education and child development.

What does this scenario augur for the voluntary sector? Probably that voluntary agencies will need to continue to provide even augment development inputs to supplement provision: step up pressure on the politicians and administrations to provide good governance: make them more responsible and accountable to citizens: exercise vigilance on issues like health and elementary education and exert greater pressure for equitable social development.

To meet the external challenges, the voluntary sector will need to introspect on its appropriate role, as providers of quality educational services to the deprived as change agents, as a protectors of child rights or as an innovators in development strategies?

In conclusion, it appears to us despite the Government being the largest sector striding the largest to smallest activity in the country, there are ever widening disquieting gaps. The resources available in the government, which could be disbursed all over, from smallest business to biggest corporates, socially spirited individuals to organized charities and in the initiatives in the villages, small towns and the big cities to the national level organizations, we are not able to garner the maximum benefits. There is definite need to associate various segments of population same as crucial sectors of activities and governance to achieve common notional goal of creating a healthy and prosperous India. Needless to mention that the success of the democratic governance ultimately rests on people's participation, whether it is organized through political leadership or the administrative machinery, through gross-root level democratic institutions, PRIs and urban local bodies, or through the million odd voluntary initiatives.

6

Voluntary Organisations' Achievements

The role of Voluntary Sector in development has been considered vital due to their vast experience and knowledge with regard to local needs, problems and resources. The commitment on the part of the Voluntary Organizations/ Non-Government Organizations (VOs/NGOs) has been considered more effective since they are not bound by rigid bureaucratic system of rules and regulations. The voluntary sector is observed to operate with greater flexibility and base its activities on the felt needs of the community. There is a growing importance for NGOs with the increased budget allocation for poverty alleviation programmes. These organizations undertake research and studies on Social Sectors such as Ilealth, Education, Social Welfare, Water Supply and Sanitation and other various government programmes and policies.

Karnataka initiatives have been taken to enunciate people's participation and involvement of NGOs in implementing several schemes of the Central and State Governments. There are more than 500 NGOs in the State. The societies, organizations, associations, trusts or companies registered under relevant Acts are considered as Voluntary Organ isations/NGOs. Informal groups like self-help groups formed under **Stree Shakti programme, Swarna Jayanthi Swarojgar Yojana. Swarna Jayanthi Shahan Rojgar Yojana** are also included under voluntary sector. Continuous efforts are being made and encouragement provided to create awareness among the public through the NGOs/VOS in rural and backward areas and urban slums in implementation of various programmes. Voluntary Organizations have been involved to organize skill development training and awareness in the fields of women and child development, social welfare, health, education, watershed development programme etc.

HEALTH AND FAMILY WELFARE PROGRAMME

National Rural Health Mission (NRHM)

National Rural Health Mission is implemented across the country from 2005 integrating Reproductive and Child Health (RCH), Immunization, Inter sectoral Convergence, Disease Control Programme etc. Under this mission, focus has been on the involvement of voluntary sector in service delivery. NGOs are participating in RCH activities like maternal health, family welfare activities, promotion of institutional deliveries, ante and postnatal care, organizing health awareness camps etc. NGOs are also involved in Reproductive Track Infection (RTI)/Sexually Transmitted Infection (STI) control programmes through Karnataka State Aids Prevention Society. RCH activities in remote and underserved areas are being carried out through 82 NGOs in 17 districts.

Several NGOs like *Karuna* Trust, JSS Medical College, Vydehi Institute of Medical Sciences have taken up the responsibility of running PHCs in remote locations. Totally 41 PHCs are run by NGOs in the state. Similarly, some district hospitals are also run on Private public participation. Provision has been made to Outsource the services of specialists in government health facilities. Institutional delivery of BPL women is taking place in accredited private nursing homes. Voluntary Organizations are also actively involved in capacity building of Accredited Social Health Activists (ASHAs) and Village Health and Sanitation Committees.

NGO are being supported financially and technically to reach and intervene with these vulnerable populations. Voluntary organizations are involved in the National Leprosy Eradication Programme. These organizations are also providing health care for special groups, which include orphanages, rehabilitation centers for the disabled/ handicapped, destitute women etc.

HIV Infection and AIDS

Voluntary organizations have helped to provide. hope in the face of the unprecedented challenges posed by AIDS. They can fill the void, tackle issues and deal with needs that others may not even recognize, or unable or unwilling to face. Many of them are involved in training, education and counselling services by sensitizing and motivating the community to take active participation in AIDS related activities, development of IEC materials etc. Some of them are also functioning as care centers.

NGOs are playing a major role in the AIDS Control Programme. There are 78 voluntary Counselling and Testing Centres in Karnataka. It has trained over 9000 health workers and initiated programmes to Panchayat Raj Institution members through satellite. They provide pre test, post test, counselling & HIV testing for Diagnosis & Surveillance purposes.

Targeted Interventions

The targeted intervention being implemented through NGOs has been successful in reaching out to High Risk Groups who are otherwise not reachable. Twelve NGOs are being supported financially and technically to reach these vulnerable populations. The main aim of the programme is to reduce vulnerability and promote safer sexual behaviours.

CBOs implementing Drop-in Centre

The care of HIV infected people is the most challenging aspect in HIV/AIDS prevention. The experience shows that to mobilize the Community Support, the advocacy among PLWHAS and networking among them for creating an enabling environment is essential. Community support groups of PLWHAS are coming forward to provide emotional and social support to themselves, such community based organizations have the committed responsibility in developing the positive attitude in the community towards individuals and families living with HIV/AIDS. Currently Karnataka State Aids Prevention Society supports five Drop-in-Centres and planning to open eight more.

PPTCT - NGOs/CBOs

Karnataka State AIDS Prevention Society is implementing the Prevention of Parent to Child Transmission programme, which is a national programme under Round 11 of the GFATM through the NGOs and CBOs across the State. The role of NGO under this programme is to motivate women in the community to attend antenatal OPDs, provide counselling on health education regarding RTI/STD, HIV/AIDS, family planning, safe sex practices, infant feeding, immunization and nutrition, community level counselling of the women and her partner on HIV testing and motivate them to visit the PPTCT centre and follow up of dropout women in the community for regular antenatal care.

NGO Activity under HIV - TB Programme:

Two NGO are working under HIV - TB Programme in eight districts and provide awareness of services of HIV and TB and home based care for IIIV positives There are 561 Voluntary Counselling and Testing Centres in Karnataka.

Education

Voluntary agencies are assisting in the department's initiatives to improve educational attainment of children. Government of Karnataka has initiated the Akshara Dasoha Program (ADP) to provide hot cooked meals to 66.15 lakh students studying in 1st to 10th standard in Government and Grant in-aid schools.

Akshara Dasoha Programme is primarily an initiative to provide food to school children and improve their health and nutrition, it is expected that the programme will also support education objectives viz. enrolment, retention, attendance and enhanced learning for those attending. This Scheme is being implemented not only by the Government Organization, but also by the Non Government Organizations. There are about 106 Non Governmental Organizations in the State who are associated in implementation of this scheme.

During the year 2009-10 a sum of Rs.45724.1 1 lakh have been allocated (State Share Rs.22298.55 lakh and Centre Share 23425.56 lakh). A sum of Rs.25215.82 lakh has been spent during 2009-10 (as at the end of Nov. 2009). Under the Scheme of the Integrated Education for disabled children, 94 Non Governmental Organizations have involved in providing education to the partially disabled children. During the year 2009-10 a sum of Rs. 1215.20 have been allocated for this programme.

Women and Child Development in India

Under Women and Child Development sector the following schemes are implemented through NGOs:

1. Santhwana
2. Scheme for care and maintenance of destitute and orphan children (destitute cottages)
3. Creches for children of working mothers
4. Hostel for girls

5. Stree Shakthi
6. Child line services
7. Fit Institutions

1. *Santhwana*

The Santhwana scheme provides temporary shelter and protection to the women who are victims of sexual abuse, rape and dowry harassment and other atrocities at home. Besides shelter and counselling, the victims are also provided with an assistance for pursuing education and vocational training for self-sustenance. In extreme cases of atrocities involving the death of the victim financial relief in the form of deposit is given to her kin; which can be encashed by she/he on attaining majority. The scheme is being implemented through NGOs in all the district head quarters and taluks. 124 Santhwana centres are functioning in the state.

2. *Scheme for care and maintenance of destitute and orphan children (destitute cottages)*

Registered NGOs working in the field of child welfare for at least three years are given financial assistance through Zilla Panchayats to run destitute cottages for the care and maintenance of orphan children, children of single parents and those from the families of below poverty line. The sanctioned strength for each cottage is 25. Expenditure on this account up to the extent of 90% is borne by the Government and the remaining 10% by the organization concerned. At present 68 destitute cottages are functioning under plan.

3. *Creches for the children of working mothers*

Financial assistance is provided through Zilla Panchayats to NGOs to start creches for the children of working women in rural areas who are engaged in agriculture and other occupations. The scheme envisages day care services viz., health care, supplementary nutrition, facilities for children to sleep, immunization, play and recreation for those in the age group of 0-3 years. The government provides financial assistance to the extent of 90% and the remaining 10% is to be borne by the organisation concerned. In all, 110 creches are functioning.

4. *Hostels for Girls*

The girls particularly from the most backward rural areas drop out of school at a very early age due to non-availability of suitable and safe accommodation at hobli headquarters or even at taluk headquarters to pursue their education. To facilitate girls from backward rural areas to pursue higher education, NGOs are provided with financial assistance to run hostels. The sanctioned strength for each hostel is 50. These hostels are located in the most backward areas of the state. At present there are 42 such hostels.

5. *Stree Shakthi*

Stree Shakti, an ambitious scheme to empower rural women financially and socially through self help groups, was launched in the state during October 2000. By the end of December 2009, 1.40 lakh self help groups have been formed. Through the self-help groups, rural women have come together and shown tremendous efficiency in handling financial matters. The scheme has empowered the rural women economically besides providing a platform for getting involved in social issues for their own benefit and also for the benefit of the community at large. As of now, there are 20.73 lakh women members enrolled in these groups. Active NGOs with expertise in the field are involved in the capacity building of selfhelp groups.

6. *Child Line Services*

The programme initiated by Government of India aims to build partnership between NGOs and society by responding to children who are in distress and in need of care and protection. The main objective of the child line services is to help children in distress by calling a help line with free toll number 1098. It provides round the clock phone services for children in difficult circumstances. The Bangalore City Child Help Line was launched with the help of Bangalore Telecom department. Child Rights Trust (CRT) Bangalore, has been identified as a nodal agency. The city is divided into three zones and operated by three collaborative agencies namely APSA, BOSCO and Makkala Sahayavani. Five more Child Lines have been sanctioned by the Government of Karnataka to the districts of Mysore, Davanagere, Dharwar, Shimoga and Bidar during the year 2009-10.

7. *FIT Institutions*

Voluntary organizations have been recognized as FIT institutions under Juvenile Justice Act for providing care and protection to deserted, orphaned infants and young children. Grant-in-aid has been enhanced from Rs.300 per month to Rs.500 per month per child vide Government Order dated 01/09/2008.

Welfare of Disabled and Senior Citizens

Around 215 VOs are running special schools for the disabled children all over the state. Of which, 30 organisations receive grants from the State Government and 95 Schools receive grants from Central _Government. Besides, 46 VOs receive grants from the State government for running old age homes, day care centres and help line for senior citizens.

Welfare of Backward Classes

232 pre-metric hostels and 17 post-metric hostels comprising 12333 and 604 inmates respectively are being run by different voluntary organizations receiving grant-in-aid from the Government. The rate of grant-in-aid provided to these VOs works out to Rs.450 per inmate per month for 10 months for pre-metric hostels and Rs.500 per inmate per month for

post metric hostels. An amount of Rs.50000 is provided as grant to different voluntary organizations for the construction of general hostel buildings. The proposals relating to training up of backward classes students by the VOs are being sent to the Central Government for sanction.

Welfare of Scheduled Castes

249 Grant-in-aid Pre-Matric hostels are being run by Voluntary Organisations for the sanctioned strength of 14456 Scheduled Caste students. State Government is providing financial assistance of Rs.450 per student per month for the maintenance of these hostels (for food charges) as per Government norms. The management committee will provide the other facilities.

90 Grant-in-aid Post-Matric hostels are being run by Voluntary Orgisations for the sanctioned strength of 7510 Scheduled Caste students. State Government is providing financial assistance of Rs.500 per student per month for the maintenance of these hostels (for food charges) as per Government norms. The management committee will provide the other facilities.

Rural Development

In Karnataka Rural Development is being pursued through state administration, local Governments and NGOs initiative. The services of NGOs are utilized in implementation of several Rural Development programmes through Grama Panchayat, Taluk Panchayat & Zilla Panchayat.

World Bank Aided Jal Nirmal-Water Supply And Sanitation

The World Bank Assisted second Karnataka Rural Water Supply and Sanitation Project "Jai Nirmal Project" is being implemented in the State for providing safe drinking water and sanitation facility for the rural population.

World Bank assisted Jai Nirmal project is a demand responsive project being implemented in 11 districts of Northern Karnataka namely Bagalkote, Belgaum, Bidar, Bijapur, Dharwar, Gadag, Gulbarga, Haveri, Karwar, Koppal and Raichur with an estimated project cost of Rs.997 crore. Water supply schemes are taken up in 744 Grama Panchayats having 3061 villages/habitations and roads and drain schemes are taken up in 1523 villages/habitations and about 51 lakh rural people have been benefited by this project. The project is proposed to be completed by June 2010.

The project is supported by NGO's/support agencies for successful implementation and also plays as a partner for community development activities. In order to achieve the key milestones under water and sanitation sector, namely adequacy, reliability, equity, quality, sustainability and self reliance, the project envisages a significant departure from conventional method of supply driven intervention to demand driven sustainable development approach, specially, capacitating Grama Panchayats and village level user groups is critical as all decision making related to planning, procurement, construction, operation and maintenance rest exclusively with Grama Panchayats and village water supply and sanitation committees (VWSCs) i.e., for providing community development and engineering including institutional and managerial support to the Grama Panchayats and village water supply and sanitation committees. In addition to this. they also have to liaison with the external agencies and to work with the Panchayat Raj Enginering divisions. NGO's are providing community development support to the Grama Panchayats. For rendering these services, 23 NGOs selected by Jai Nirmal Project have been paid Rs.7.55 crore during 2007-08, Rs.2.37 crore for the year 2008-09 and Rs.1.18 crore for the year 2009-10 (Up to September 2009) which includes the payment towards Support Agencies also.

As at the end of December 2009, 2847 water supply schemes and 1427 roads and drain schemes have been implemented. Remaining water supply and roads and drain schemes are under different stages of progress.

State Government has released a sum of Rs.83600 lakh as at the end of December 2009 since inception and against this Rs.84081.39 lakh (including the Community & Grama Panchayat contribution and accrued Bank interest) is utilised. As at the end of December 2009 Rs.65609.45 lakh has been claimed as reimbursement since inception and out of this Rs.64883.64 lakh Additional Central Assistance is cleared by Government of India.

Suvarna Gramodaya

His Excellency The President of India has launched the Suvarna Gramodaya Yojane on 25.2.2007. This is a new initiative of the Government of Karnataka for developing vibrant village communities by adopting an intensive and integrated approach to Rural Development. The new initiative will focus on the development of 1000 villages every year by the concerted efforts of the Government, Non-Governmental Organisations, Private sector partners and the Village communities.

The specific objectives of Suvarna Gramodaya are as follows.

(a) To upgrade the physical environment of the selected villages for improving the quality of life

(b) To fully develop the income generating potential of land based activities.

(c) To provide full and adequate infrastructure for human resources development including education, health services, and child care facilities etc.

(d) To generate significant levels of non agricultural employment, especially for educated unemployed youth

(e) To support community awareness and development through self-help groups, cultural associations etc.

Preparation of Village Development Plans

The entire programme of Suvarna Gramodaya is being implemented on the basis of detailed village development plans prepared for each village. The district officials incharge of the programme will select appropriate Non-Governmental agencies to prepare a socio-economic profile of the village and specific development plans for each village. The draft plans will be discussed with the village community and the Grama Panchayat and their suggestions are taken in to account before they are finalised. The district officials will then approve the plans for implementation.

7

Strength, Weaknesses of Voluntary Sector

Voluntarism is a phenomenon of ancient Indian society, where people shared skills, expertise, services, resources and knowledge among the members of communities living together. In the present era, voluntarism manifests through organizations, associations; organized structures such as Community Based Organizations, Voluntary Organizations

> ***Voluntary Organization***
>
> A voluntary organization is a non-governmental, autonomous, non-profit making organization supported mainly by voluntary contributions in cash and kind from the general public or certain segments of the public, specialized to carry out a number of functions related to development, aid and emergency relief.
>
> The main characteristics of voluntary agencies would be that they:
>
> - be established by a group of private individuals or NGOs;
> - be autonomous;
> - elected periodically by the membe rs;
> - have a clearly defined constitution and be accountable to that constitution;
> - be financially independent;
> - have a formal legal status, permanent headquarters and employ professional or volunteer staff; and
> - have humanitarian objectives and programmes.

(VOs), Non-Government Organizations (NGOs), etc. From charity, relief and welfare oriented activities, voluntarism has suitably moulded itself to undertake development activities in keeping with the needs of the.time and society.

Voluntary Organizations in India, particularly in some States, are creditably rendering support in supplementing the efforts of State Governments towards community mobilization, social change and economic development by virtue of their mobilization Endeavour, contacts and linkages with the people of far flung and inaccessible areas. Although 4.21 lakh, voluntary organizations are registered in Uttar Pradesh, the number of voluntary organizations with good reputation in their sphere of action is very. limited. The culture of voluntarism has not as yet permeated the society in Uttar Pradesh in the manner it has elsewhere.

In spite of improvements in the levels of development in Uttar Pradesh, the traditional methods of implementing various schemes, which depend largely on Government's efforts, are facing many short-comings. Some of these are as under:

- Experience of implementation of several development programmes show that the reach of services in rural areas is poor.
- Benefits of development have not percolated down to the poorest of the poor.
- Administrative overheads often consume, the major part of financial allocations leaving little for services.
- Health services and primary education continue to be characterized by qualitative and quantitative deficiency.
- Diversification in agriculture is yet to pick up pace.
- Steps for empowerment of women, SCs/ STs/ OBCs in terms of organizational support and programme implementation have to be strengthened.
- Soil conservation, land recovery, watershed development, greening of the environment, cleaning of rivers, rural development and slum development

schemes are areas where voluntarism and participation can matter. These are areas that demand social mobilization and stakeholders' involvement in voluntary modes.

- Inefficient functioning of all-important infrastructure.

The above mentioned illustrative deficiencies have to be overcome. That would demand Innovative approaches and strengthen voluntarism. Voluntarism, civic responsibility and participatory development process are expected to generate awareness, reduce inefficiencies and contribute to sustainable development. In addition, voluntarism promotes

Strength of Voluntary Organization

- Dissemination of knowledge regarding local conditions and close communication with the local communities enabling them to assess local needs of the people and motivating them and enlisting their ready participation in the development programmes.
- Flexibility of approach, less role bound, no rigid guidelines as in the government departments. This enables them to innovate, do action research and come out with the strategies I really related to local needs.
- Less complex administrative structure as compared to government departments.
- Much closer to the poorest section of the society and they interact with the section directly across the table.
- Use of local resources.
- Committed to achieve local self sufficiency
- involvement of women in the voluntary agencies programme
- Access to unpaid or less paid workers.
- They can provide more efficient delivery of services at substantially lower costs and create gainful employment.

interaction with people and leads to the right identification of problems and formulation of appropriate strategies for solving them.

It is a sound choice of policy, made by the planners to promote voluntary action in programme identification, planning and implementation in decentralized modes. In addition, efforts are being made to improve the working of

Weakness of Voluntary Organization

- A Their inability to cooperate with each other.
- Their accountability and transparency is not proved by and large.
- Their operations are small in scale.
- Uncertainty over availability of human and financial resources hampering planning of their activities

voluntary organizations by helping them in improving their capabilities, scaling up their operations and by making their selection and working more transparent and accountable.

Voluntary sector in the State

The details of voluntary organization in the State such as NGOs, SHGs, Mangal Dals and the Departments / International Agencies implementing their schemes with the help of voluntary organizations are given below:

A-Non-Government Organization (NGOs)

According to Registrar Firms, Societies and Chits, Uttar Pradesh, 4.21 lakh NGOs were registered up to March 2005 for charitable purposes and for the promotion of Khadi and Village industry, Panchayat industry, Rural Development, Science, Education, Health etc. Departments like Medical and Public Health, U.P. Health System Development Project, SIFPSA, Welfare of Child and Women, Agriculture, Bhumi Sudhar, Diversification of Agriculture, Drinking Water and Sanitation, Social Welfare, Labour, Rural Development and Panchayati Raj are implementing several schemes with the help of NGOs.

B-Self Help Groups

State Departments /agencies like Rural Development, Bhumi Sudhar Nigam, DASP, Women welfare are implementing their Departmental schemes with the help of Self Help Groups. In the State, 3.341akh Self Help Groups have been constituted up to

March 2004 by various departments. Some of the Groups formed, are being registered as NGOs for rural development works by Bhumi Sudhar Nigam.

C-Yuvak Mangal / Mahila Mangal Dals

Yuvak Mangal / Mahila Mangal Dals are being formed in the State by the Yuva Kalyan Vibhag at Nyay Panchayat level. 0.32 Lakh Yuvak Mangal Dal and 0.28 Lakh Mahila Mangal Dal were formed in state up to July 2005. Yuva Kalyan Vibhag is encouraging Mangal Dals to get them registered under Societies Registration Act 1860 for various activities related to the Sports, Forestry, Family Planning and small saving etc. So for 0.29 lakh Yuvak Mangal / Mahila Mangal Dals have been registered.

D-International Agencies

In addition to the NGOs, SHGs and Mangal Dals certain International Agencies such as CARE India and UNICEF etc., are also working in the State for implementing their externally aided schemes with the help of selected NGOs. CARE India is implementing its schemes through 17 selected NGOs in rural areas and 1 3 selected NGOs in urban areas of the State.

Voluntary sector in the various Five Year Plans

In the history of development planning in the State, the first model of community participation was put into practice during the First Five Year Plan. Since then, it has been continuously recognized that the right place for any development activity to take place, is the grass-root level. The Third Five Year Plan emphasized that "the concept of public cooperation is related to the much larger sphere of voluntary action in which the initiative and organizational responsibility rest completely with the people and does not rely on legal sanctions or the power of the State for achieving its aims."

During the Fourth and Fifth Plan periods, the thrust on public cooperation and involvement of people's organizations lost pace due to external aggression on the country and economic recession. Role of voluntary organizations in the development process got a further fillip in the Seventh Plan when it was declared that serious efforts would be made to involve voluntary organizations in various development programmes to supplement governmental efforts and to offer the rural poor, choices and alternatives. This emphasis continued till Ninth five year plan.

Strategy for the Tenth Five Plan and Annual Plan (2006-07)

Recognizing the important catalytic role played by the voluntary sector in the socio-economic development of people particularly those living in the un-served areas, one of the major strategies of the Tenth Plan is to promote voluntary action in far-flung and inaccessible remote rural and city slums as they are the only medium to reach the unreached. The voluntary organizations in the State, are being encouraged in the field of Education, Technical Education, Health, U.P. Health Systems Development Project, Family Planning. Women and Child Welfare, Watershed, Diversification of Agriculture Project. Bhumi Sudhar, Forest Department, State Drinking Water and Sanitation. Social Welfare, Labour Welfare, Rural Development and Panchayati Raj during the Tenth Plan and the Annual Plan (2006-07).

So far, a number of steps have been taken by the State Government to create an enabling environment for the Voluntary Sector and multiply opportunities for their vigorous collaboration in the implementation of various developmental and welfare programmes. Some of the important measures taken by the State Government in this direction include:

- Norms/guidelines for selection of voluntary organizations were finalized by the State Government. Under these guidelines, greater emphasis is given to the transparency, merit and equal opportunities in the selection of voluntary organizations.
- Establishing State Advisory Committee headed by Chief Secretary for examining the rules/laws related to VOs and other policy level decisions.
- Declaring Planning Department, Government of U.P. as the nodal department to coordinate and interface between VOs and Government.
- In order to facilitate and give a strong push to voluntary action in the fields of development planning, community mobilization and capacity building, a NGO Cell has been established in the Planning Department with following objectives:
  a) To act as a nodal agency for State Government-voluntary sector interface.
  b) To prepare the data base of voluntary organizations working in the State.
  c) To act as a facilitator for increasing the scope and reach of institutionalized voluntary group and promote their people-friendly working.
  d) To streamline the selection procedure of voluntary organizations and make it transparent for implementation of development /welfare programme.
  e) To coordinate the training needs between voluntary organizations and the concerned user department of the State Government.
  f) To evolve Monitoring and Evaluation systems for programmes being implemented by voluntary organizations.
  g) To promote wider dissemination of the success stories of voluntary organizations and to promote programmes for their replication.
  h) To evolve Model 'Code of Conduct' for V O's

Three committees were constituted in the NGO cell to review the present status and also to suggest methods, measures and action- steps to be taken thereon to convert the above mentioned objectives of NGO cell into real practice. These committees included the representatives of various users departments and Non-Government Organizations as Chairpersons / members. On the basis of recommendations received from the aforesaid Committees, the State Government is in the process of evolving a State Policy for the Voluntary sector. This is expected to be finalized during the current financial year.

Major features of the proposed policy are as under:

- Sensitizing Government officials about the catalytic role of voluntary organizations in the process of development planning.
- Review of policies and simplification of procedures / guidelines for involvement of voluntary organization.
- Strengthening the Data-Base of voluntary organisations on the basis of this territorial functioning, sources of funding, work expertise and potential.
- Review of Societies Registration Act, 1860 to suit the needs of people as also User Department.
- Encouraging voluntary organization to serve in un-served remote areas.
- Evolving transparent and common system for the selection and funding of the Voluntary Organization for different Departments / organizations.
- Evolving Code of Conduct for the voluntary organizations in which accounts and physical progress will be made available to concerned Gram Sabha. This will also help in bringing about transparency in the functioning of the voluntary sector.
- Identification of good and bad voluntary organizations. Wide publicity of such information using the web site of the Planning Department.

- For monitoring and evaluation of schemes / programmes being implemented by the NGO, it is proposed to form a "District Monitoring/Evaluation Committee" under the Chairmanship of District Magistrate. It is also proposed to link physical progress with the payments procedure in a judicious way.
- Government – voluntary organization interface through periodic interaction with the help of the NGO Cell, to remove grievances and improve functioning.
- Identification of Mother NGOs for capacity building of voluntary organizations. Monitoring the budgetary provision for training of NGOs by various Departments.
- Documentation and dissemination of success stories for replication of best practices used by voluntary organizations through wide publicity using the Planning Department's website and other media means.
- Studying the level of coordination between government and NGOs in various States for experience sharing and adoption of good practices.

During the Ninth Five Year Plan, Planning Department allocated for the first time an outlay of Rs.168.56 crone for voluntary sector against which an expenditure of Rs.86.54 crone was incurred. The proposed outlay for voluntary sector in the Tenth Plan (2002-07) is Rs.736.51 crone. In the Annual Plans of 2002-03, 200304 and 2004-05 an expenditure of Rs.54.44 crore, Rs.32.17 crone and Rs.23.35 crone respectively has been incurred. Similarly, against an outlay of Rs 14.73. crone during the Annual Plan 2005-06, the anticipated expenditure is Rs.6.36 crone. The proposed outlay for the Annual Plan 2006-07 is Rs.14.51 crore. The sector-wise details are given in the following table.

Outlay and Exp enditure or Voluntary Sector (Rs. in Crore)

Sectors	Ninth plan 1997-2002		Tenth Plan 2002-07 Outlay	Annual Plan 2002-03 Exp.	Annual Plan 2003-04 Expen-diture	Annual Plan 2004-05 Expen-diture	Annual Plan 2005-06		Annual Plan 2006-07 proposed outlay
	Outlay	Expen-diture					Proposed Outlay	Anti-cipated Expen-diture	
1	2	3	4	5	6	7	8	9	10
1. Agnculture (UPDASP) Pase-I & II	-	10.40	628.74	6.00	0.77	5.31	10.00	-	0.72
2. U.P. Sodic Land Reclama-tion Project			19.63	2.76	2:28	3.18	4.07	1.19	4.13
3. Water Supply and sanitation	131.43	75.58	67.50	34.78	24.41				
4. Women Welfare	5.23	-	15.92	4.82	1.79	0.50	-	0.51	
5. Welfare of SC/ST/DT	31.90	0.56	4.00	0.48	0.01	0.39	0.66	0.66	0.66
6. Social Welfare	-	-	0.72	-	-	-	-	-	-
7. Nutrition	-	-	-	5.60	2.91	13.97	-	4.00	-
Total	168.56	86.54	736.51	54.44	32.17	23.35	14.73	6.36	14.51

8

Challenges in Voluntary Sector

View of the Voluntary Sector

India is a welfare state. Therefore education, health and social welfare are the responsibility of the state. In late 60's and early 70's, a new breed of organisations called "Voluntary Organisation". Now they are known in many names. They are:

- Non-Governmental Organisations (NGOs)
- Non-Profit Organisations (NPOs)
- Not-for-profit Organisations (NPOs)
- Voluntary Organisations (VOs)
- Non -Governmental Development Organisations (NGDO's)
- Government Promoted NGOs

There are many differences between "Non-Profit Organisation" and "Profit Organisation". We need to understand that non-profit organisations are not debarred from earning profit. The key difference between a 'Non-Profit Organisation' and 'Profit Organisation' is in its purpose of existence. Whereas 'Profit Organisations' exist to earn profit, for "Non-Profit Organisation", profit comes as incidental to its operations. Secondly, in profit organisation, the surplus/ profit is distributed among the owners/ shareholders of the organisation. In a non-Profit organisation, the surplus is used to further the objective of the organisation.

The main sources of receipts for voluntary organisations are:

- Self Generated Funds
- Grants
- Donations
- Membership Fees (subscription)
- Surplus from Business

Activity As per a study conducted by John Hopkins University on the voluntary organisations, there are 1.2 million voluntary organisations in India. There are million people e associated with voluntary organisations paid or voluntary staff. Approximately, 20,000 crore rupees are Mobilized from within and outside the country in a year. About 5,000 crore rupees are received as foieign contribution every year. There are about 30,000 FC(R)A registered organisations in India.

Key Issues

The social and economic development the country. Voluntary organizations have been able to reach the remote corner of the country braving adverse situations. Voluntary organizations have also been known for exemplary selfless service to the !ess privileged and marginalized sections of the society.

Inspite of all these the voluntary sector suffers from lack of clarity and operational difficulties in its accounting, reporting, management and legal franrework.

- Legal framework and Governance
- Accounting and Reporting
- Income Tax
- FCRA

Legal Framework & Governance

Voluntary organizations can be registered broadly in three ways. They arc:

- Registered Public Charitable Trust
- As a Charitable Society
- As a Not-for-Profit Company (Sec.25 of Companies Act 1956).

Each of them have their own issues to deal with.

Registered Public Charitable Trust

Indian Trust Act, 1882 is not applicable to Public Charitable Trusts. Therefore, Public Charitable Trusts are registered as a Trust under General Law with guidance from:

- Charitable & Religious Trust Act 1920.
- Religious Endowment Act 1863.
- Bombay Public Trust Act 1950.

The trust deed is only registered. As a result. once these organizations are formed. there is no mechanism within the frame work of the law to regulate them. The only exception being the states of Maharashtra. Gujarat and Goa where there is charity commission. But a very little facilitation for trusts is observed. They have to be registered under Income Tax Act, 1961 when they seek Income Tax exemption and, under FCRA, 1976, if they apply for foreign contribution. But the basic regulatory mechanism for public charitable trusts is not there. Therefore, it is entirely left to the organisations to make necessary practices and procedures for good governance.

Charitable Societies

Charitable Societies are registered under Societies Registration Act, 1860. On one hand, the Act is very . old and in some sense has outlived its utility. On the other hand, there is every poor administration of the Act. Then there are different requirements for different States as there are State Acts as well. For example, in the state of Karnataka, the Act requires that 1% of the total receipts for the year is paid as filing fees along with the annual return of the society for the year. In the State of Uttar Pradesh and in some other States the registration is available for only five years and then it has to be - renewed. Since many of these offices of Registrar of Societies are not computerised, it is very difficult to know the status of the returns of any society. Therefore, the Registrar of Societies plays a very little regulatory role for Societies. In this scenario, it is difficult even to get data about the actual member of active NGOs registered under the Act. Since there is no real compulsion to dissolve the organisation once the members are not actively pursuing its objective, therefore there are plenty of dormant NGOs.

Not-for-Profit Company (u/s 25 of Companies Act, 1956)

This form of registration is by far the best regulated. The Registrar of Companies is quite active in regulating entities registered under the Act. However, since the reporting requirements are more. small and medium sized organisations find it difficult to cope with it.

Accounting & Reporting

The accounting legislation applicable to NPOs do not lay down the form of balance sheet and the requirements as to income & expenditure account. Even there are no requirements for additional disclosure. As a result of which these issues are left to the judgement of the accountants and auditors. Therefore, we can see todav that there are many annual accounts of NPOs which do not even have previous years figures, leave alone disclosure practices.

There are no specific accounting standards for NPOs in India. The Institute of Chartered Accountants of India has come out with "Technical Guide on Accounting and Auditing in Not-for-Profit Organisations". The guide strongly recommends:

- Maintenance of books as per accrual basis;
- NPOs should follow the accounting standards irrespective of whether any commercial, industrial or business activity has taken place.

However, we must note that there are certain areas very much NPO specific which have been left un-explained. For example, NPOs raise a lot of non-cash local contribution. The accounting and reporting of it is a major challenge before the sector. The Income Tax Act does not recognize non-cash contributions and therefore they have to be kept outside of the return for income tax. The FCRA requires a Receipt & Payment Account and Balance Sheet. This again implies that the non-cash contributions need not be reported to FCRA authorities as well.

The second example is treatment of restricted fund. The restricted funds are not the income of tire organisation as they are for a pre-determined purpose and the NGOs do not have any control over it, Therefore. a clear direction from ICAI on this issue will be helpful.

Thirdly, ICAI strongly suggests accrual basis of accounting for NTOs. It also needs to come out with a practical guide on ways to implement it in an organisation. There would be issues like grants due but not received, corresponding expenses etc.

Fourthly, ICAI also needs to suggest certain disclosure norms for NPOs as well as standardized form of Balance Sheet and fund based accounting statements (instead of Income & Expenditure Account.

Income Tax

Under the Income Tax Act, 1961, the NPOs are not required to pay tax if they follow certain reporting requirements.

However, NPOs are facing certain operational difficulties under this Act as well.

- Until the year 2001, the NPOs were able to accumulate income tip to 10 years and spend it within that period. However, in the Finance Act, 2001 the 10 years period was reduced to 5 years.
- In the year 2002. accumulation of income which was earlier allowed up to 25% of the total income was reduced to 15%. Further InterCharity donations out of accumulated funds were also not allowed.
- Now in 2006, Section 115 BBC was inserted according to which any charitable organisation receiving anonymous donations would be charged to tax at the maximum marginal rate.

We can see that systematically certain privileges which were earlier available are being withdrawn. This is a cause for concern. Whereas as an NPO there is no doubt that it would be committed to highest level of accountability, certain amount of space need to be provided for it to perform better, Another issue that comes up is that India becoming the hub for development in South Asia, there is a need for mobility, of funds within South Asian countries. As per the Income Tax Act, at present, the funds can be utilized only within India to be eligible for exemption from Income Tax.

FCRA

FCRA was enacted in the year 1976. Therefore it is now, 30th year of the implementation of the Act. Being an internal security legislation, this is under the Ministry of Home Affairs. There are few issues/concerns which need to be addressed for smooth functioning of the sector.

Bank Accounts

There needs to be a clarification from the FCRA department authorities about multiple bank accounts, As per the Act, only one designated bank account can be opened for receipt of foreign contribution. However, it is not explicitly stated that for utilization, there can be more than one bank account even through practically, it is implied that an organisation cannot operate with a single bank account for implementation of its programme given the fact that the actual operational area may be far away from the place where FCRA designated bank account is situated. The draft Foreign Contribution (Management & Control) Bill, 2005 makes it explicitly clear that multiple bank accounts are allowed for utilization of foreign contribution. Therefore, it may be deduced that the intent of the law makers is to allow multiple bank accounts for utilization.

The second issue under bank account is the change of designated bank account. It may be helpful to stipulate a timelimit for disposal of the application for change of designated bank account. This will help many NGOs who struggle with certain inefficient banks to operate their designated bank account and are apprehensive to approach the FCRA department to change last they have problem with their FCRA registration.

Change of Office Bearers

On 27.12.1996, the Form FC-8 was changed which includes a declaration by the Chief Functionary to give an undertaking which among other conditions, specifies that foreign contributions should not be accepted if more than 50% of office bearers as mentioned in the application at the time of registration are replaced or changed. This is not valid for organisations registered before 27.12.1996.

This declaration in certain ways limits good governance. One of the ways of promoting good governance is rotation/ term of board members. Therefore, this declaration needs to be removed to enable organisations to be better governed.

Time Limit for regular registration

Presently, there is no time limit prescribed under the Act to approve or reject the application in Form FC 8 for regular registration. It is important that a time limit is prescribed for disposal of application for regular registration.

Foreign Contribution (Management & Control) Bill, 2005- Few Concerns

The draft Foreign Contribution (Management & Control) Bill, 2005 which was put in the public domain for discussion has thrown up some very serious concerns for functioning of NGOs. Some of them are:

Renewal of registration every five years;

Fixing of Administrative Cost,

Disposal of Assets

9

World Civil Society: At A Glance

By 1970 the rise of civil society and the diminishing role of the state, was under way throughout the world as well. Loss of faith in government was a phenomenon witnessed in many countries, most dramatically with the Watergate scandal in the United States, which climaxed with the president's resignation in 1974. But this was not an isolated incident.

In many parts of the globe, civil society was asserting itself, willing to challenge the authority of the state and to undertake tasks the latter was either unwilling or unable to perform. In the democratic states of Europe as well as in the United States and Japan, political commentators began discussing the question of governability – the ability of the state to cope with the increasing demands of society.

There was less and less optimism that the government had the will or the capabilities to do so; ehnce their increasing willingness to turn to civil organizations to share the task. All in all, then, *state-society relations* were changing rapidly, both within individual countries and in world affairs as a whole. Perhaps it was no accident that religious bodies, especially the Catholic Church were beginning to regain the influence in domestic political and social affairs, as fi to reclaim the influence they had lost to the secular authorities.

Even some countries that had not hitherto tolerated anything close to a civil society began to witness the emergence of nongovernmental associations, thanks in no small degree to the encouragement and support that the Church provided. An informal group of intellectuals in Chechoslovakia founded in 1977 to call for respect for *human rights*, was one example, and Poland's labor organization, Solidarity, offered another. Established in 1979, the latter started out as a trade union of Gdansk dockworkers led by Lech Walesa. But, as an association outside the government or the Communist Party, it soon attracted a membership totaling some nine million and became a model for similar organizations in other socialist states.

In the Soviet Union and elsewhere, students, intellectuals, and dissidents grew steadily bolder and began to organize themselves. Their associations, many of them clandestine, may not have been exact replicas of nongovernmental organizations in democratic countries, but they were clearly becoming self-conscious members of a civil society that was emerging in Eastern Europe.

Indeed, the concept of civil society came to be developed during the 1970s as representing forces that were not controlled by the state. Those involved in the construction of nonstate organizations in Eastern Europe were conscious of the international implications of what they were doing. They were in increasing contact with developments in the West, the European and American capital was beginning to be invested in the Soviet Union and elsewhere to produce larger quantities of consumer goods.

There is little doubt that for intellectuals, journalists, labor leaders, and others in these countries, freedom of association came to be seen as a key aspect of contemporary Western society and that they believed this was where they would have to start to become part of global developments.

Civil society also grew outside Europe, although the impetus for the growth of nongovernmental organizations seems to have been more social and economic than political. In Latin America, Asia and Africa. Large number of voluntary agencies sprang up to cope with problems of poverty, hunger, and health to complement work by the public authorities. Often governments were too weak, corrupt, or inefficient to administer social services, and they willingly turned these tasks over to non-state bodies.

Why their number should have begun to increase during the 1970s is unclear, but it is remarkable that so many community organizations that are active today seem to have originated at that time.

Perhaps the world economic disaray of the early 1970s hit particularly hard those Third World countries that were not endowed with rich natural resources. It may also have had something to do with the spectacular rise in cross-national migration.

Driven by civil strife, ethnic conflict, and poverty, millions crossed borders, often illegally. Fortunate ones found refuge in richer counties of Europe, North America, Oceania, or the Middle East, but a greater number ended up in refugee camps. In Africa, for instance, the number of refugees grew from three hundred thousand in 1960, to one million in 1970, and to over three million ten years later.

Even among those who stayed home, sprawling slums were a common sight in larger cities. Voluntary work was often the only effective means fo dealing with such a critical situation. Small-scale community organizations were founded, and successful ones inevitably grew larger as they expanded the scope of their activities. Even such organizations, however, held political connotations inasmuch as they were involving people the poor, women, and other marginalized groups in community affairs. They were engaged in grassroots, bottom-up efforts in contrast to the top-down pattern of governmental programs for relief and economic development.

Thus, in many instances community organizations served to empower people who had hitherto been deprived of a voice in their *own governance*. From there, it was but a step to an active campaign for their rights.

Such a development seems to have exemplified many nongovernmental organizations in the Third World during the 1970s. Thus in the non-Western parts of the world, too, self-conscious civil society was emerging.

Nor was the growth of civil society in many parts of the world limited to domestic organizations. *Branches of international nongovernmental* organizations were established everywhere, their total number increasing from 36,336 in 1966 to 52,074 in 1977, and to 79,786 by 1983. In 1977 the Soviet Union belonged to 43 international nongovernmental organizations, and China to 71. These were much smaller figures than the number of international nongovernmental organizations in United States (1,106) or in Japan (878), but they were nevertheless indicative of a trend. The figures for Africa, the Western Hemisphere, and Asia (including the Pacific) for that year were 6,830, 11,076, and 9,725, respectively.

It was almost as if the whole globe was becoming dotted with domestic and international nongovernmental organizations. Added to them were *local offices of intergovernmental organizations,* totaling 6,432 in 1977. These number show that global consciousness was becoming even more fully institutionalized than earlier.

The new international order that was being promoted at the geopolitical level through the rapproachement between the United States and the Soviet Union, and between the former and China, had its counterpart in the emerging global community consisting of thousands of intergovernmental organizations and international nongovernmental organizations, as well as of domestic civil societies.

It is no accident that astute observes of the international scene began to notice this phenomenon. Some of the seminal works on international organizations were published during the 1970s. In 1975 Johan Galtung, a leading scholar of nonstate actors, argued in a pioneering essay, "Nonterritorial Actors and the Problem of Peace," that a "sixth continent" of the world, "the invisible continent of nonterritorial actors," was emerging.

Two years later, Evan Luard, a British student of international politics, published *International Agencies*, a guide to the existing *intergovernmental organizations* that is still useful. The important work by these and other scholars were summed up and put into a comprehensive framework by Harold K. Jacobson, whose *Networks of Interdependence* (1979) may be considered the basic text for the study not simply of *international organizations* but also of *international relations* in general during the 1970s. As he wrote in the preface, "Humankind is crafting new political institutions that have already contributed significantly to greater global security, to better material welfare through a larger gross world product, and to higher standards of social welfare."

All these authors were noticing a global development that would soon enter the consciousness of millions of people everywhere: the proliferation of international organizations, some of which expanded on the work begun earlier, while others were innovative in that they were not elite bodies but were products of, and responses to, the political, social economic, and cultural concerns of the individual.

10

Human Rights and NGOs

We have seen that these five, plus peace and disarmament, had been among the most important objectives of international organizations. While peace advocacy was by no means inactive, the easing of Cold War tensions may have had the effect of eclipsing it as a central issue for international organizational attention.

According to Margaret Keck and Kathryn Sikkink, twenty international nongovernmental organizations were concerned with peace issues in 1963, but the number declined to fourteen ten years later. Further fluctuations would occur in the years to come, and while generalizing may be impossible, one could argue that the five fields just mentioned were now considered more urgent.

If such a generalization is tenable, it underscores the fact that beginning in the 1970s, so many issues outside of world peace and arms control came to command the attention of people everywhere, who were increasingly seeing that the solution to these problems lay in international organizations, not sovereign states.

To start with human rights, one remarkable development during the 1970s was the increasing attention that began to be paid to women's rights. The years 1975 to 1985, according to the historian Harriet Alonso, were "ten years of unprecedented global organizing" among women's groups. These years were designated by the United Nations as the "International Decade of Women," with 1975 as "International Women's Year," an indication that at both nongovernmental and inter-governmental levels, women's movements were becoming an important part of any discussion of world affair.

While such a widened perception of international relations had become notable during the cultural revolutions of the 1960s, the new decade added significant elements to the phenomenon. For one thing, even outside Western Europe and North America, where women's organizations had had long histories, similar movements developed to such an extent that in 1975, an international congress of women was convened in Mexico City. Not surprisingly, the participants resolved to create networks of women's conditions and lifestyles varied from country to country and from one culture to another, but the common sentiment was that by coming together, women's group from different parts of the globe could develop a common consciousness – a consciousness of shared concerns and commitments.

This was reflected in the publication, starting in 1975, of *Women's International Networks News*, a quarterly journal of information, and in the first "international tribunal on crimes against women," held in Brussels in 1976. This was not a formal trial in the ordinary sense of the term, but an occasion where two thousand participants from forty countries aired their grievances concerning violence against women, including rape and prostitution.

Such development may suggest that while women's international movements had initially focused on peace issues, especially against nuclear armament, the easing of Cold War tensions during the 1970s enabled them to deal with other matters as well, and in so doing, women's organizations became more than ever an integral part of the emerging phenomenon of globalization.

For instance, the establishment in 1974 of a new organization in the United States. Women for Racial and Economic Equality, suggests that marginalized and disadvantaged segments of the population could join forces with women everywhere to search for a new order at home and in the world.

Human rights, in that broad sense, were becoming a major theme of international affairs. three disparate episodes would demonstrate this graphically. One was the 1975 Helsinki accord on human rights, adopted at a meeting of the Conference on Security and Cooperation in Europe (CSCE), a body that had just been organized by members of the North Atlantic Treaty Organization and the Warsaw Pact. The creation of the CSCE was itself a major landmark in postwar international history.

Significantly, the declaration defined *human rights broadly* and referred to "the rights of the individual to know and act upon his rights."

That such a principle was never wholly accepted, let alone practiced, in socialist regimes was less important than that the nations belonging to opposite sides in the Cold War now put their signatures to the same document, indicating that they were willing to embrace common values regarding the human condition.

In 1978 Helsinki Watch was established to monitor the signatory nations' compliance with the 1975 agreement. In that process its staff met, often clandestinely, with dissident individuals and groups, thus encouraging the growth of civil society in the Soviet Union and East European countries.

Another interesting example concerned the rights of those who were physically, mentally, or otherwide disabled and had traditionally been subject to harsh discrimination in many societies. The United Nations' universal declaration on human rights had not asserted the rights of the disabled.

At last the world organization made amends when it issued a declaration on the human rights of the mentally disabled in 1971 and another, encompassing all types of disability, in 1975.

These declarations called on all countries to improve the conditions of such people. Hitherto, religious organizations, especially various Catholic orders, had been conspicuous because of their attention to the disabled, considering them to be God's special children, but now in many parts of the world, disabled persons and their relatives and friends began to establish organizations to lobby their respective staters for more support, financial and moral.

In the United States, for instance, people with disabilities asserted their rights as consumers: they should, they insisted, have the right to choose their own rehabilitation programs, hospital and institutional care, and welfare facilities.

Similar movements developed elsewhere, and in time awareness grew that the disabled should organize themselves internationally. The first international nongovernmental organization of the disabled, disabled Persons International, was not founded until 1981, but in the meantime worldwide awareness of their existence and problems was aroused through international sporting events.

Although the first Paralympic games had been held during the Rome Olympics of 1960, and the second in Tokyo in 1964, it was during the 1970s that such activities became more truly international. In 1969 the Stoke Mandeville Sports Stadium for the Paralysed and Other Disabled was opened in Aylesbury, Britain, and in the following year an international competition was held there, attracting four hundred physically disabled athletes from twenty-eight countries.

Soon such events came to include the blind and those with cerebral palsy, and in the meantime the mentally disabled began to have their own "special Olympics." The 1980 Olympics for the Disabled, held in Arnhem, the Netherlands, drew twenty-five hundred competitors from forty-two countries.

Such as even could not have taken place without the painstaking preparation by a large number of volunteer organizations, and it reflected the fact that *human rights during this period* were broadening to encompass the well-being of people with disabilities.

A third illustration of the growing influence the human rights question was having on the world was the award, in 1977, of the Nobel Peace Prize to Amnesty International.

Since its founding in 1961, the organization had rapidly established branches in various parts of the world and widened the range of its activities. It was particularly active in sending observers to prisons to ensure proper treatment of inmates. When, in 1975, the International Council of Nurses declared that "the nurses in the care of detainees and prisoners" must report all instance of "physical or mental ill-treatment," Amnesty International made sure that such a rule was enforced.

It also took seriously a declaration by the World Medical Association at its convention in Tokyo in 1975 that obligated doctors "not to condone, countenance, or participate in torture." That most countries of the world were willing to let Amnesty personnel visit their prisons indicates the tremendous authority this international organization was already beginning to assume in international affairs.

Given the rising global concern with human rights, it is not surprising that the United State government under the presidency of Jimmy Carter (1977-1981) responded to the situation by establishing a bureau of human rights and humanitarian affairs within the State Department.

The bureau was headed by the assistant secretary of state for human rights and worked energetically to promote democratization. Although Carter's human rights diplomacy was criticized for its lack of consistency – for instance, he insisted on democratization of South Korea, but not as firmly in China or in Pakistan.

International organizations, not separate states, provided consistency. Where governments could pay only limited attention, nongovernmental organizations made sure that pressure would be kept up on behalf of incarcerated political dissidents and other victims of discrimination and injustice. A great deal of cooperation in this regard also existed between intergovernmental and nongovernmental organizations.

The United Nations Center for Human Rights, for instance, was in constant communication with international nongovernmental organizations and was receiving information from them on abuses of human rights in many parts of the globe. Private foundations in Europe and North America, notably the Ford Foundation, for the first time came to interest themselves in funding international human rights work.

11

International NGOs

All such activities in the human rights field did not mean, however that international organizations were neglecting other areas of their traditional and recent concern. In the broad area of humanitarian relief, for instance, the United Nations International Children's Emergency Fund (UNICEF) continued to be active in providing health services to children and their mothers.

Some seventy million people were reportedly being served by clinics equipped by UNICED in the mid-1970s. *Among international nongovernmental organizations* were some notable newcomers, such as Africare and Food for the Hungry International, both established in 1971. The former complemented work by older institutions such as Project Concern International and worked closely with the World Health Organization and other *intergovernmental organizations to provide medical service* and health care facilities in remote areas of the African continent.

African's initiative for its founding came from African leaders (such as Diori Hamani, president of Niger) who appealed to African Americans for help. C. Payne Lucas, director of the Peace Corps Office of REturned Volunterrs in Washington, took up the challenge and started the project, initially headquartered at this home with a small budged of less than forty thousand dollars. At first envisaged as a relief organization to help victims of drought in West Africa, it soon came to embrace a more ambitious, long-term goal, to offer developmental assistance.

Food for the Hungry, in the meantime, was founded in southern California (and later moved to Arizona) as "an international organization of Christian motivation, committed to work with poor people to overcome hunger and poverty through integrated self-development and relief programs." Soliciting donations from other countries as well as the United States, the organization helped refugees in Bangladesh (which separated itself from Pakistan in 1971), earthquake victims in Nicaragua, and the hungry in West Africa. It also created a Hunger Corps to send volunteers volunteers to administer food distribution programs in cooperation with local organizations.

In 1976 a new organization was set up in London, the Appropriate Health Resources and Technology Action Group, to serve as a repository of information concerning public health research and administration. Around this time, the notion of primary health care became incorporated into the vocabulary of international organizations.

At an international conference convened by the World Health Organization and UNICEF in Alma-Ata in 1978, attended by representatives of 143 countries as well as sixty-seven international organizations, a declaration was issued, asserting the rights and duties of people everywhere to participate in primary health care "in the spirit of self-reliance and self-determination." "Health for All by the Year 2000" was adopted as the goal toward which nations and international organizations were to strive.

No international nongovernmental organization founded during the 1970s in the field of humanitarian relief has been as well known or influential as Doctors without Borders (Medecins san Frontieres). Its creation in 1971 owed itself to the initiatives of a handful of volunteers and donors (mostly in France) who were committed to the idea that humanitarian activities recognized no national boundaries and that physicians and nurses should go wherever they were needed to help victims of famine, disease, or natural disasters. (The phrase "without frontiers" was so attractive to other organizations that in France alone, more than thirty of them adopted it as a part of their names.)

As a founder of the organization wrote, in this way it was frankly "subversive"; it would not always wait for, or go through, government authorization before acting, and it would not hesitate to publicize its activities or the plight of the people it assisted.

During the 1970s, doctors and aid workers dispatched by the organization became involved in relief work in Nicaragua after an earthquake, in vietnam after the long war, in Thailand to provide assistance to refugees from Vietnam and Cambodia, and in several African states to care for refugees fleeing civil strife.

In such activities, Doctors without Borders often frankly confronted the issues of human rights and was willing to disseminate information on violations of those rights. The line between humanitarian relief and human rights activism was thin. The Alma-Ata declaration spoke of the principle of making primary health care accessible to "individuals and families in the community through their full participation." People's involvement in their own health care, and more broadly in their own development, was being asserted as a right, but this could come into conflict with local political ambitions and traditional prejudices. From the beginning, volunteers working for Doctors without Borders and other organizations encountered situations in which the implementation of humanitarian activities experienced difficulties in the absence of a system of governance through which individuals could assert their rights.

In such instances, they would have to organize themselves as autonomous entities – something state authorities would not easily tolerate. But it was becoming clearer that the more humanitarian agencies involved themselves in the local scene, the greater the challenge to the existing framework of state sovereignty.

Thus here, too, the growth of civil society was emerging as an inevitable by-product of international humanitarian work.

The same was true of developmental assistance. The 1970s witnessed a continued growth in the number of international organizations in this field. This clearly reflected that the rising cost of energy and the fierce trade competition that resulted from it were making the economic conditions of developing countries worse than ever, relative to those of more advanced countries.

The former came to be known collectively as the "South," and the latter as the "North," and it seemed as if the North-South rift was becoming even more serious than the geopolitical conflict between East and West.

As many Third World countries found it difficult to obtain revenue by marketing their primary exports, whose prices tended to be depressed throughout the decade, they began pressing for what they called a "new international economic order" in which their special circumstances would be given consideration and their products given preferential treatment. Because the governments of the richer countries would make only partial concessions in this regard – for instance, exempting such products from international agreements on mutual lowering of tariffs – private groups would naturally become more deeply involved than ever in providing developmental assistance.

Many of them were organized in France where, as earlier, the Catholic Church expanded the scope of existing organizations and created new ones to extend assistance programs to former French colonies in Africa and in Latin America.

One of them, the Comite Catholique contre la Faim et pour le Developpement, devised a slogan, "Rien ne changera dans le tiers monde si rien ne change chez nous" (nothing will change in the Third World if nothing changes at home).

Such a view expressed the recognition that developmental assistance made sense only in the context of a world that was becoming closely interconnected and in which values such as freedom, justice, and human rights applied everwhere, at home as well as abroad. For this reason, developmental assistance programs and projects came to have an important human rights component, another remarkable phenomenon of the 1970s.

We can see this, for instance, in the founding of the Centre for Development and Population Activities in 1977 in Washington (with field offices and "partner organizations and networks" in many countries), aimed at "empowering women at all levels of society to be full partners in development."

As the insertion of the word "population" in its title suggests, this organization stresed women's reproductive health and family planning as essential aspects of economic development. These were politically sensitive issues, and, as noted later, the growth of multiculturalism, a parallel development in the same decade, would make them extremely controversial. Of interest to our discussion is that social and cultural questions were becoming inseparable from developmental assistance.

In 1971 a Consultative Group on International Agricultural Research was launched at the behest of the World Bank and of several governments and nongovernmental organizations. Initially designed to help agricultural research, especially in rice production, the Group soon became involved in broader issues such as farming systems, conservation of genetic resources, and other phenomena that had "ecological, economic and social factors."

Also about that time the World council of Churches established a "program to combat racism" to help individuals and groups in Portuguese Africa as well as Rhodesia and South Africa that were struggling against colonialism and racism. Oxfam America, founded in 1970, often criticized the United States government for its aid policy that seemed to help existing regimes entrench themselves in power instead of promoting the well-being of ordinary citizens. Reflecting a similar concern, the Society for Internationa Development adopted "jobs and justice" as its objectives for the 1970s, justice being defined as a concept including "cultural diversity and safeguarding the environment."

Cultural diversity and the safeguarding of the environment – these two themes were beginning to claim the serious attention of governments and nonstate actors alike during the 1970s, another distinctive characteristic of the decade's international relations. Not just in connection with humanitarian relief or developmental assistance, but with regard to many other issues, the two subjects were entering into the vocabulary of national and international discourses. Understanding why is not diffucult.

To discuss environmental protection first, by the early 1970s this issue was apprently becoming urgent, given the polluted skies and waters in so many parts of the world, products of rapid industrial development and population growth during the preceding decade. "Defoliation" and "desertification" were now familiar terms; renowned forests such as the Black Forest in Central Europe began to lost their trees as a result of atmospheric pollution, and deserts spread in Africa because of overgrazing and other causes (including climatic change, although there was no consensus on this point), causing havoc with animal habitats and food shortages for humans.

In many cities of the world, as more and more people gained sufficient incomes to own a car, not just gasoline consumption but also air pollution from automobile exhaust grew.

Diseases, physical impairment, even deaths were reported in different parts of the world as a result of poisoning by mercury and other industrial chemicals. When nations steadily switched to nuclear power, a move that seemed essential to reduce their dependence on petroleum, they encountered the problem of protecting themselves against radiation.

The connection between environmentalism – the concern with hazards to the biosphere caused by economic activities – and developmentalism was clear. As more and more countries undertook industrialization, they encountered the same environmental issues the plagued the more advanced nations.

Would development and environmental protection be compatible? That was becoming a major issue of international affairs. Most Third World countries insisted on the imperatives of economic growth, to remove themselves from the indignity of perpetual poverty. And yet the vocabulary of environmentalism was such that unlimited growth appeared less and less a desirable end – so it seemed to some observers among the already industrialized countries.

Such vocabulary came into conflict with the increasingly popular view that it was precisely because the more advanced countries had enriched themselves by relentlessly exploiting the resources of the poorer lands that the earth faced an ecological crisis. Furthermore, some factories from industrialized nations were relocating themselves, partly to take advantage of cheaper labor in Third World countries but also to escape environmental regulations at home.

That such factories might be "exporting dirty air" to less advanced countries was a charge that began to be made in the 1970s. But that did not mean that these lands should remain in a perpetual state of underdevelopment. Here was the dilemma. How could nations promote both development and environmentalism?

Soon the world would become familiar with the concept of sustainable growth, a pattern of economic development in all nations that did not overburden the earth's resources or injure its biosphere.

It was in the 1970s that the potentially explosive issue of environmental protection was first addressed internationally, at conferences and through new organizations. Despite the deeply divisive nature of the issue, there was agreement that this was a worldwide problem and therefore had to be dealt with in a global framework. A landmark event in internationalizing environmentalism was the United Nations Conference on the Human Environemt, convened in Stockholm in 1972.

A product of the UN resolution of 1968 calling for such a gathering, the conference attracted representatives from 114 countries. The gathering was often contentious, as could have been predicted, but remarkably the delegates adopted a resolution calling on the United Nations to establish a special body to deal with environemental issues through international cooperation.

The recommendation resulted in the inuguration, in 1973, of the United Nations Environmental Program. This body became a major forum for defining international environmental policy in connection with developmental assistance. Third World countries insisted, and developed countries usually agreed, that the enforcement of environmentally sound programs should not be at the expense of the former's sound economic development or trade, and that the costs of instituting such programs should be largely borne by the richer nations.

The objectives of environmentalism and developmentalism could come into conflict, but the new international organization served as a forum where such differences could be aired and, to the extent possible, ironed out. This was a perfect example of the impact of new issues upon international governance.

The Stockhold conference produced almost immediate results in Europe, where the European Community was being established through the addition of Britain, Ireland, and Denmark to the original European Economic Community.

From its beginning, the European Community took environmental issues seriously. Through the European Council, the Community's ultimate governing body, the member governments adopted environmental action plans and, at the same time, began coordinating their plans so as to develop common regulations for environmental protection.

In the meantime, the European nations as well as others organized a large number of conventions throughout the 1970s dealing with such specific issues as "the prohibition of the emplacement of nuclear weapons and other weapons of mass destruction on the sea-bed and the ocean floor and in the sub soil there-of" (1971), "the prevention of marine pollution by dumping from ships and aircraft" (1972), "international trade in endangered species of wild fauna and flora" (1973), "the protection of animals kept for farming purposes" (1976), and "the conservation of migratory species of wild animals" (1979). These agreements testified to the willingness of sovereign states, particularly of Europe, to give up part of their national prerogatives to cooperate in pursuit of common objectives.

While national governments became increasingly interested in environmental issues, nongovernmental organizations that had already been active in the field redoubled their efforts, and many new organizations were established during the 1970s. Some of them were represented at the Stockhold conference, while others held their own meetings apart from the United Nations-sponsored gathering. Their agendas were not always compatible, but their presence demonstrated that they could not be ignored in any discussion of environmental problems. The Stockhold conference provided an occasion for internationalizing the activities of many national nongovernmental bodies concerned with the environment. As of 1973, according to a survey, ten international non-governmental organizations existed in this field, one of the most influential of which was Friends of the Earth, established in the United States in 1969. Its founder, David Brower, had been active in the Sierra Club but felt that this and other conservationist groups were not resisting strongly enough pressures from business and governmental offices for "wise uses" of natural resources. Rather than reform such associations from within, Brower and other decided to create their own organization, which from the beginning would be global in scope. During the 1970s, Frends of the Earth branches were formed in many other countries to disseminate information and campaign actively for the preservation of the natural environment. After the Stockhold conference, additional organizations were created, so that within ten years the number of environmental international nongovernmental organizations reached twenty-six. In 1974 the Center for International Environmental Information was established in New York, and six years later its name was changed to the World Environment Center, a clear indication of the globalizing trend of such activities. These organizations grew so numerous that in 1975, a conference was held in Austria to review the relationship among them, as well as between them and the United Nations, in administering environmental and related social programs.

One of the most energetic and successful organizations founded during this period was the Antarctic and Southern Ocean Coalition, formed in 1977 to try to preserve the Antarctic region from oil drilling and excessive fishing. Its representatives began to lobby nations participating in the Antarctic treaty system, a collection of treaties that governed this area. The Coalition eventually won the right to send observers to these meetings, and in the meantime, they engaged in a worldwide campaign to preserve the Antarctic. Although many political and legal issues complicated their activities, especially regarding the enforcement of any international agreement, the organizations was tireless in publicizing the critical situation in the region and promoted, among other objectives, the negotiation of a convention on the conservation of Antarctic marine living resources. Their efforts were to be rewarded in the early 1980s when such a convention was adopted and became part of the treaty system.

The protection of endangered species was an integral part of environmentalism. The safeguarding of wildlife from human encroachment had a long history, but during the 1970s international nongovernmental organizations became even more conspicuous than before in speaking out against the killing of elephants, whales, and a variety of animals, birds, fish, and plants. When various individuals and organizations spoke of the "quality of life," an increasingly popular phrase, they meant not simply that of humans but also of all living beings that shared the "planet earth," another increasingly used term. Reflecting such a trend, the World Wildlife Fund, the International Union for the Conservation of Nature and Natural Resources, and other organizations that had been founded earlier were now more successful than before in persuading national governments and intergovernmental organizations to take wildlife protection seriously. For instance, in 1972, the World Wildlife Fund, in cooperation with Friends of the Earth, spearheaded a campaign to save whales through newspaper advertisements and street marches in London. (That the Duke of Edinburgh was by then president of the WWF gave the movement much greater visibility.) In response, the British government imposed a ban on the import of products made from baleen whales. This was far from being a complete victory for whale conservationists, and some of them were to move on to become Greenpeace activists. The growing influence of all these nongovernmental organizations is remarkable all the same.

An interesting development of the 1970s was that the preservation of the natural environment was often coupled with that of historical and cultural landmarks. In 1972, at a UNESCO meeting in Paris, a "convention concerning the protection of the world cultural and natural heritage" was signed by seventy-five countries. The United States was the first nation to ratify the convention.) The coupling of cultural and natural resources showed that culture and nature were beginning to be seen not as opposites, as had long tended to be the case in many parts of the globe, but as closely integrated so that talking of preserving one at the expense of the other would be impossible. An emerging perspective of this period saw culture and nature as interdependent. Moreover, rapid economic growth in many parts of the world had caused serious damage not only to nature and wildlife but also to ancient monuments and work of art. Just as endangered species needed protection, rare historical artifacts had to be treated with care lest they should disintegrate. According to the 1972 convention, individual countries were to prepare a list of historical landmarks within their borders, from which a number would be registered with an international committee on historical preservation. The latter would compile a master list of the world's most precious historical heritages, and those that required immediate care would be provided with funds for restoration and protection. The assumption was that these cultural monuments, just like the natural habitat, belonged to the whole of humanity, and that it was the responsibility of all people to ensure both natural and cultural preservation.

The growing popularity of the notion of multiculturalism, another interesting development of the 1970s, may be said to have been an aspect of the concern with the preservation of historical heritages. Multiculturalism con-noted the idea that culture must be seen as pluralistic, consisting of divergent ways of dealing with the human condition. Just as the preservation of pristine oceanic conditions and endangered wildlife was a moral imperative for the whole world, respect for different ways of life and thought came to be seen as an important agenda for international affairs. Pleas for cross-cultural understanding had long existed and produced many important movements and organizations dedicating themselves to a myraid exchange programs. And during the 1960s, a sense of transnational cultural consciousness had emerged. But during the 1970s, multiculturalism gained even greater influence because of its conjunction with other developments such as the rise of global environmentalism and the worldwide mushrooming of non-governmental organizations. Here were forces pushing for globalization – the term began to be used toward the end of the decade – but the growth of global consciousness was also giving rise to awareness of diversity. Globalization and multiculturalism as twin themes – this was an idea that would eventually come to seem commonsensical. In the 1970s the picture was not yet so clearly recognized, but even so, individuals and organizations promoting educational and cultural exchanges were becoming keenly aware of the connection.

The continued growth of exchange programs during the 1970s and subsequently tends to be overlooked by students of international organization because of their fascination with the more dramatic activities by advocacy groups, such as those concerned with human rights and environmentalism. Purely in terms of number, however, exchange organizations continued to overshadow these other associations. International organizations promoting educational and cultural exchanges grew just as rapidly as the latter, and together they contrinuted to strengthening transnational networks.

For one thing, the 1970s saw significant developments in exchange programs between the two sides in the (already waning) Cold War, as well as between the West and the People's Republic of China. In 1971 UNESCO began the World Scientific and Technical Information Service to provide bibliographic information on published articles, numbering over one million a year, in seventy thousand specialized journals, which provided an opportunity for scientists from the Soviet Union, China, and other socialist countries to join the international community of scientists. The 1975 Helsinki accord contained the so-called Basket III, which dealt with cultural relations and endorsed exchange programs between NATO and Warsaw Pact countries. About this time, cultural exchange between socialist and capitalist nations picked up mementum. For instance, American and Soviet scientists began collaborating in energy and space research, as exemplified by the *Apollo-Soyuz* joint space mission undertaken in 1975. Two years later, two Soviet historians co-authored a book, an account of the history of U.S.-russian relations, that was published by the University of Chicago Press; while the book struck many american reviewers as biased, its very publication indicated that the transnational interchange of ideas across ideological divides was becoming accepted.

Likewise, the rapproachement between the United States and the People's Republic of China after 1971 reopened channels of communication between the two that had all but disappeared during the preceding two decades. The Committee on Scholarly Exchange with the People's Republic of china, which had been set up in 1966 under the auspices of the National Science foundation in anticipation of the resumption of scholarly contact, now established a Beijing office to oversee the renewed exchanges. In cooperation with the Council for International Exchange of Scholars, the Washington organization that administered the Fulbright program, the Committee served as a liaison between Chinese and American students, academics, and professionals as they visited each other's country. On the Chinese side, the Chinese Academy of Social Science, a Beijing organization, played the key role in hosting visiting Americans and coordinating plans for scholarly cooperation. At this time such cooperation was still very limited, but at least the beginnings of the U.S.-Chinese cultural exchange, coming on the heels of the worldwide cultural revolution of the 1960s, served to make international intellectual cooperation and communication more nearly global than had been the case earlier. Moreover, in the United States and elsewhere, new nongovernmental organizations sprang up with a focus on the promotion of exchanges with the People's Republic. Foundations, universities, and professional societies began establishing offices and training staff to serve this purpose. While no exact counterpart to such organizations existed in China, these private initiatives from abroad sowed the seed for what would soon blossom into a large-scale exchange between the Chinese and the rest of the world.

That the growth in the number, scope, and diversity of international exchange programs was giving rise to serious questions may be seen in the fact that during the 1970s, the governments of the United States, Britain, France, and Germany commissioned studies to reexamine their respective cultural policies. In the United States, an "independent panel on international information, education and cultural relations," funded from private sources, recommended that the dissemination of information about the nation should be combined with exchange programs under a single administration. For this purpose, the United

States Information Agency was renamed the United States International Communication Agency, starting in 1978. Although the former name was restored after only four years, the stress on communication and exchange, not just on information, was to remain. This change reflected the recognition that the spread of information as an aspect of Cold War diplomacy was now of secondary importance compared with the sharing of ideas and experiences with all countries. In the meantime, an officially sponsored review undertaken in Britain recommended, in its report of 1977, that the British Council be either abolished or scaled down. Such a radical idea was more in response to severe economic problems at home that the product of a new view of international cultural relations, and the government did not accept the recommendation. But the review did reflect the growing sentiment that cultural affairs could mostly be left in private hands rather than officially promoted. In any event, the official response to the report pointed to the importance of "educational and cultural work" in "stimulating the use of the English language" abroad.

This, apparently rather mundane, point was becoming a matter of serious concern to French officials concerned with cultural affairs. A report written in 1979 by a committee headed by Jacques Rigaud acknowledged that English had overtaken French as the language of international communication. The report suggested that France's cultural heritage and ideas could be promoted by languages other than just French. The world was changing, the report pointed out, because of "the involvement of people in international affairs," and it was therefore imperative to consider French cultural centers abroad as places of exchange with the local populace. This did not mean that the teaching of French in other countries should be neglected, but that the training of teachers of French abroad should be emphasized, linked to the concept of *francophonie*. A German report, published by the Foreign Ministry in 1978, admitted that German was not an international language, but it was even more emphatic that the documents of the other countries in stressing the significance of "international cooperation in the cultural sector" so as to "create ties between people of different nationalities." Echoing the French report, the German statement asserted, "All nations are today, more than ever before, dependent on one another for their existence.... The value of what we give is only worth as much as our willingness to take. Thus, an open attitude towards others is a principle of our cultural policy abroad."

It was against such a background that organizations, national and international, faced the issue of cultural diversity. Those espousing multiculturalism insisted on the autonomy of each culture, defined by religion, ethnicity, race, gender, sexual orientation, and other factors. The world, in such a view, consisted of a variety of specifically definable cultures, each with its own values and agendas. No one culture was inherently superior to others. To the extent that one culture, for instance Western civilization (characterized by exponents of multiculturalism as having traditionally been dominated by white males), tended to claim superiority (or "hegemony," another word gaining currency), it must be rejected. To push such an argument to its extreme, multiculturalism would deny the existence of universal truths or values; all cultures were equally valid. The validity or authenticity of a culture must be recognized before constructing any device for cross-cultural communication and cooperation.

Such an assertion presented a serious challenge not only to cultural exchange but also to human rights, environmentalism, and a host of other causes that were being promoted by intergovernmental organizations and nongovernmental organizations. If there were no universal human rights or a shared commitment to the protection of the natural habitat, how could a global community of men and women with common interests and agendas develop?

Was it ever possible to conceptualize such a community to begin with? Was not the idea itself a hegemonic one, coming from a dominant civilization to impose its definition of the world on others? If the globe was becoming subdivided into self-defining cultures with their own local loyalties, should communication and dialogue among these cultures be even attempted? Was a multicultural world compatible with a viable international civil society?

These were serious questions, and they added complexity to international affairs in general and to the workings of international organizations in particular during the 1970s. The very idea of cultural exchange came to be assaulted as a product of Western civilization, even a maneuver by the powerful European and North American countries to hang on to their position of worldwide influence. Although during the 1950s UNESCO had stressed humanity's diverse cultural heritage and sponsored conferences on Eastern and Western values, the assumption was that dialogue was possible and desirable among such diverse heritage and civilizations. All countries and cultures, cultural internationalists had believed (and continued to believe), shared a commitment to mutual communication and understanding. During the 1970s, however, some of the more outspoken leaders of Third World countries began to insist that they did not necessarily share Western ideas about such matters, and that any attempt at cross-cultural cooperation must reflect their perspectives also. Some intellectuals – among the most influential was the Algerian writer Franz Fanon, whose book *The Wretched of the Earth* (1965) was among the first systematic presentations of the argument – asserted that their first task was to liberate themselves from the cultural vocabulary that had provided them with words and concepts to comprehend the world, indeed to describe themselves. The time had come, they argued, for them to develop their own vocabulary if they were to be fully independent of the colonial past. Similar ideas were expressed in a scholarly fashion by

Edward Said, the American scholar of Palestinian background, whose *Orientalism* (1978) became something of a bible of multiculturalism. In such a perspective, freeing Third World people from their dependence on the West for knowledge and information would be vitally important.

These views were aired at UNESCO and other international settings, making cross-cultural exchange a far more complex undertaking than earlier. Some observers considered the situation so serious as to nullify all attempts at international cultural cooperation. Add to this the rise, in the late 1970s, of postmodernist theory, which argued against the ideas of progress, modernization, and evolutionary historical process but stressed the essential meaninglessness of concepts, terms, and words, except in the context of the individual uttering (or hearing) them. Postmodernism could present a serious intellectual challenge confronting all attempts at global community by intergovernmental and nongovernmental organizations.

The crisis would continue into the subsequent decades, but remarkably it did not prevent the further promotion of international exchange programs. The governments of the United States, Britain, France, and Germany continued to recognize the importance of cultural and educational exchange, although they were also aware of the need to refine and reformulate their exchange programs to cope with the challenges of the age. The 1970s saw many new initiatives undertaken by these and other countries, both officially and privately, to promote communication and understanding among nations. In 1971, for instance, the European Federation for Intercultural Learning was established as the umbrella organization of American Field Service offices thoughout Europe. These offices had been engaged in providing "home-stay" experiences for young people as a way to foster transnational learning and understanding. In the United States, many programs designed for encouraging cross-cultural understanding were created, such as the

Educational Resource Development Trust, the Educational Foundation for Foreign Study, and Friendship Force. All were established during the 1970s to bring Americans into closer contact with people elsewhere, especially from non-Western parts of the world. In 1977 the Fulbright Association was founded in Washington to facilitate interaction among former Fulbright scholars. And in 1979 the International Student Exchange Program was organized to provide funding and logistical support for interchange among American and overseas students and young faculty members.

Even among European nations that had been traditionally active in cultural exchange programs, there were so many of them that in 1976, a conference of cabinet ministers in charge of cultural affairs was held in Oslo to coordinate European cultural exchange. In the meantime, the French-American Foundation was established to initiate a program of exchange professors between French and American universities, while the German Historical Institute opened its offices in Washington, London, Tokyo, and elsewhere to undertake cultural exchanges. And in 1972 the Japan Foundation was created by the Ministry of Foreign Affairs to encourage the development of Japanese studies abroad as well as the exchange of scholars, artists, journalists, and many others between Japan and other countries. Around this time, research organizations, or think tanks, began to be set up in Japan, after the pattern of those in the West. The National Institute for Research Advancement was one of the first such organizations, and from the beginning it engaged in projects that were predominantly international in character.

12

The Future of Voluntarism

'Voluntary action' should not be seen merely as another form of action. Rather, it is woven into the very structure and ethos of Indian society – more a way of life than a form of action. It is closely tied to the fundamentally plural nature of our society. In India pluralism is not just a characteristic of the political system as in the case in Western polities; it is something ingrained in the very structure and organization of society.

Indian society for centuries survived the vicissitudes of history without a centralized political system. Except for short periods, it lacked a clear centre. Even those short period had a rather limited rach and proved to be transitions in the long march of Indian civilization. The core of the civilization was cultural rather than political. Its 'State' was intermittent, scattered and multipolr, an arena of conflicting claims of a large number of clans and regimes. The real 'action' was by voluntary entities representing trade and commerce and the 'mahajans' governing them, and cultural, religious and caste and caste-like organizations. The view often held by Westerners, that India consisted of a series of republics, represents a misreading of this voluntary, non-political, non-State cultural terrain.

Today, at the end of 50 years of state-sponsored and directed effort at resolving problems, we seem to have come a full circle. Once again the State is losing both its capacity and its legitimacy, and both opinion and action seem to be veering round towards voluntary thinking and action. Of course, not all voluntary effort is a result of reaction to State directed policies and institutions.

In its core manifestations, voluntay effort is initiated by diverse individuals and groups; its distinctive features lie in its being autonomous, relatively independent and self-propelled. Indeed, as one surveys the Indian reality, one finds that a large part of innovative and creative endeavour in many fields is voluntary in nature, not a result of external incentives. Thus, if one says that voluntarism has been an enduring feature of India, it only means that many people at many places are engaged in multifarious action without being asked to do so by an external agent–political, bureaucratic or market-propelled.

The perception of a dichotomy between State-directed and voluntary initiatives has arisen only in recent decades *after* the modern State and its institutions either began to impede the voluntary ethos of Indian society or forced themselves on what people did on their own. The contemporary interest, both scholarly and political/ bureaucratic, in voluntary action has arisen because of this imposition, for long accepted as beneficial but which in the long run has proved to be largely (though not wholly) inimical to people's interests with the result that large sections of people are once again forced to rly on their own methods of resolving their problems. Not that this is always to their liking. Often they are compelled to fend for themselves, whereas they would have liked to participate in the formal structures of the modern State, to benefit from the opportunities it promised to offer. Hence the recurring image of voluntary action as a response and reaction to the failure of the State and its policies and programmes. However, even while returning to the voluntary terrain in ways that may appear reactive, we are soon likely to discover a more positive and liberated sense of what voluntarism involves.

The model of development which we adopted on achieving Independence–and for which we 'fought' during the freedom struggle–was one in which the government was seen as the key to social change and to improving the life chances of the mass of the people. Unfortunately, the focus of the movement became merely 'capture of power' from the British. This largely meant capture of governmental powr, not *swaraj* in its full-blown sense as was conceived by Gandhi and other leaders of the movement.

Political Development vs. Social Emancipation

There was, however, a school of thought which gave priority to social reform, viz., the early liberals as well as the later radical thinkers engaged in social emancipation of the oppressed classes, who considered it to be more important that any premature rush for political independence. Ambedkar was foremost among such leaders, as were Phule and other predecessors of his. There were others too, such as M.N. Roy, for whom waging a war against fascist tendencies at both global and national levels assumed greater importance than any formal transfer of power from the British to the Indians.

In the model adopted, not only was the government central to bringing about social change, so too was a conception of 'democracy' in which political parties were to be the basic units for choosing those who were to be in power and who were to be in opposition. In structuring the relationship between the institutions of governance and the people, this model relied essentially on parties and the party system in which elections were to play the main role. Similarly, a new set of political parties were seen to provide alternatives to the prevailing order fashioned by the 'ruling' party.

Thus, both for creating a consensus on critical issues and for challenging current policies and ideological positions, parties were meant to be the key actors. The people were left to exercise choices between given sets of parties and their candidates. There was no provision for them to initiate the process themselves or even to participate in the selection of candidates. They were expected merely to put their mark on the ballot paper consisting of names of candidates selected by political parties. They were not even given the choice of rejecting all the candidates proposed.

In fact, the only decisive role that the voters have is to reject a government in power. They have little say in what the incoming government or party (or coalition of parties) is to do. They have in effect little say in the governance of the country in any positive manner. The only rights that they enjoy are of a negative kind. This is what the model of governance and dissent that we gave to ourselves upon becoming independent has brought us to. This model has increasingly led to discontent and disillusionment with the operating system over the last quarter of a century Also, it has, over time, produced a response wholly different from what was provided by parties in what, several years ago, I, along with others, had conceptualized as the non-party political process.

Such a response, in which critical though small segments of intelligentsia and a slowly expanding community of social activists played an important role, led to the proliferation of voluntary organizations in large parts of the country at both micro- and macro-levels. Many of them operated at the very grassroots, while some of them engaged in either networking these micro efforts or in setting up voluntary institutions which were distinctly political and espoused a particular ideological line.

Not all the micro efforts at voluntary action are, however, political. Some of the macro efforts too are of a non-political nature. Indeed, some of them deliberately keep away from the political process, particularly the voluntary organizations with a Gandhian origin or those of the liberal vintage, which chose instead to focus. on certain ethical norms or the defence of civil rights. At the other end of the spectrum are groups that take a more radical and often 'revolutionary' stance-from the Naxalites to the regionally-based militant fortnatiotas found in Punjab, Kashmir and the North-East and in a different way, those offering sustained resistance to State repression and armed assaults of the upper classes in Andhra Pradesh, Bihar and parts of Maharashtra. Together, the 'voluntary sector' consists of diverse groups engaged in a variety of activities and forums of assertion ai and espousing varied causes, and yet somehow together presenting a challenge to the political and economic model that continues to inform the Indian State and its key institutions (the executive, the legislatures, the judiciary, the mainstream mass media and the party system)

Alongside the growth of non-party and non-governmental action was a highlighting of a series of issues not confined to a mere expression of dissent and protest. Examples of these various issues include: the state of the environment, the condition of women, preservation of tribal and other ethnic identities and resistance to their displacement and eviction as a result of the building of large dams and thermal plants, the arena of deat politics following growing atrocities and violence against them, struggles against different forms of social exploitation such as bonded labour, position of migrant labour and the horrendous condition in which children and especially the girls are placed (a good part of the women's struggles also dealt with violence against women).

Movements vs. NGOs

As struggles on these issues gained strength, voluntarism emerged in a new form of 'movements'. It took two shapes —specific movements such as the environment movement, the women's movement, the dalit movement, and the movements of the tribals, and, a broader networking of issues through macro formations such as the Jan Vikas Andolan, the Bharat Jan Andolan, the Azadi Bachao Andolan, and the most recent and comprehensive of them all, the National Alliance of People's Movements.

Simultaneously, the non-party and non-governmental organizations have also been metamorphosing into what are called the NGOs, currently the most widespread form of voluntary action. This is partly because several developments at the international level have given rise to the emergence of a new corporatist model of capitalism. Institutions like the World Bank, IMF and WTO; major UN bodies such as UNDP, UNICEF and FAO; and donor agencies are showing a preference for the transfer of technology, develolpment funds and in some instances even finance capital to NGOs at the national and local levels alongside governments. Similarly, a series of international 'summit' conferences on envirornnent, human rights, population, social dimensions of development (known as the social summit) and women have all been followed up by massive transfer of funds to NGOs, either directly or through ministries in national governments.

This new constellation of 'voluntary' effort, encompassing funding agencies and international NGOs, units within government bureaucracies and the Planning Commission meant to assist national and local NGOs provides a completely new model of both joining in and containing, co-opting and corrupting the large mass of genuine, grassroots based, activist efforts. Whether this NGO model of voluntarism will further accentuate the great divides between the haves and the have-nots, or ameliorate the condition of the latter, is still an open question. It will depend on how the people respond to them, just as the fate of the dominater model of governance will depend upon how the people, increasingly getting disenchanted and alienated with it, will respond to it over time.

On this depends the future of voluntary- action in India. Many of the voluntary, non-governmental and non-party responses to the established order, led by activists and in some cases backed by radical intellectuals, have also been sought to be incorporated in the NGO framework, gradually losing their militant and dissenting stance as well as their pursuit of an alternative political process. However, some of them still continue, despite difficulties, to launch struggles on behalf of the poor and marginalized social strata.

While the activist arena is entering this ambivalent phase, a new upsurge of both consciousness and action from the grassroots has been under way, which, if successful, may lead to highly innovative strides towards genuine voluntarism. It consists of the rise of the poor and the oppressed themselves (not just on behalf of them as is the case with the activists), who are tired of waiting for the system to deliver the goods. They are already showing their disdain for parties and governing elites, who prefer to take advantage of the increasingly regionalized and decentralized structure of the Indian polity and who, far more than the urban middle class, have found a stake in the democratic political process and are participating in large numbers ill it. As this process gains ground, they would be willing to challenge the established institutions and replace them with not only a new system of governance and representation but also a new model o' organizing civic affairs.

For this they will need to draw increasingly upon their owl confidence, their ecological resource base, their ethnic; caste-like, tribal and other indigenous identities; all this as part of engaging in the transformation of the system. This is both in terms of moving away from the Western-inspired models of governance and competition and in terms of giving greater salience to the institutions, systems of knowledge and technical know-how which had evolved over the centuries but had been allowed to wither under the impact of imported and alien ideas of organizing society, economy;

polity, administration and laws Much of this is still in its very early stages and there is likely to be a considerable backlash from established elites and global structures

Rise of New Voluntarism

To reiterate, voluntarism has, over the centuries, been the hallmark of Indian society. The new upsurge that I have talked of here holds the promise of returning our country and our culture to its basic genius. But we live in an uncertain world and therefore face an uncertain future. Much will depend on how we respond to not only the political crisis that we face but, even more importantly, the intellectual crisis generated by the collapse of all ideologies and the all-round erosion of self-confidence. Fortunately, there are still a number of conscientious men and women who can take up the challenge, along with literally thousands of others—women and youth in particularwho would be willing to join them in creating a social order that is at once elevating and rooted.

Whether or not they will succeed in creating such a social order will depend on their ability to move along the course indicated here with speed and confidence. Many forces are at work with which the prevailing system has not been able to cope. This period of erosion of parliamentary institutions, parties and the authority of the State and of the national political leadership has also seen the rise of new actors on the scene, a new style in the conduct of public affairs, and new definitions of the content of politics.

There has also been an upswing of a new form of voluntarism, not non-political (as was the case with the voluntary bodies that were set up soon after Independence) but political in a way different from the parties, aiming at ends different from the mere seizure of State power. In the process they are helping to redefine both the meaning of politics and its ideological moorings and concepts like revolution and social transformation (including archaic notions like class struggle). Also implicit in such a redefinition is a conception of politics that is multidimensional. It is no longer limited to economic and even narrowly conceived political demands but it seeks to cover ecological, feminist and cultural aspects, including a sustained attack on sources of 'internal' decay and degeneration, including within the voluntary sphere itself. Only thus can we return to the holistic conception of swaraj, which was conceived as not just a struggle against an external power but also against internal structures of exploitation, apartheid and exclusion.

The essence of such a transition has to be a new order based on a new consensus. The political system and its socio-economic counterparts that were put in place by the Congress after Independence, though based on a consensus, were soon overtaken by the Westerninspired (Nehruvian?) model of development and the attempt to centralize power and homogenize the diversity of cultures. Fortunately; the scope for dissent and expectations for change built into the Congress system and the democratic process in course of time called for the need to restructure the consensus.

Political consensus is an on-going process, it has to be revived constantly and provided with new meaning. Democracy poses both an opportunity for creating and recreating consensus and a challenge to its mechanical continuation based on what is called the 'demand explosion' of our times. The new turmoil among the Indian masses, like the new forms of expressing demands through engaging in protest and struggle, is part of the continuing commitment to democracyindeed a further deepening and broadening of its base. It needs to be located in the larger context of a world in transformation, to be seen as an expression of new stirrings of consciousness engulfing large sections of society, a new conception of rights and responsibilities. It also signifies a new understanding of the democratic process, moving from an almost exclusive preoccupation with parties and elections to deeper currents of change involving millions of people.

Only thus can the new voluntarism become a catalyst of human liberation and genuine freedom. In its absence, mere voluntary action arising from the erosion of the modern State and its institutions can easily degenerate into uncontained violence or other forms of anarchy and decay and disintegration which may once again pave the way for an authoritarian or fascist intervention. If the new voluntarism is to prepare the ground for people's empowerment in a genuine fashion, for the exercise of freedom with responsibility, and a conception of justice that is available to all, it will need to bear in mind that the new consensus on which it is based will need constant renewal through the exercise of 'eternal vigilance' on the part of all. This will have to be a continuous process for there is no conception of any end product in such a vision of an unfolding fiture.

Bibliography

Agarwal, Anil Darryl D'Monte and Ujwala Samanth (eds) (1987), *The Fight for Survival: People's Action for Environment,* New Delhi, Sage Publication.

Agnes, Flavia (1992a), *Give us this Day our Daily Bread, Procedures and Case Law on Maintenance*, Bombay, Majlis. "Maintenance for Women: Rhetoric of Equality", Bombay, *Economic and Political Weekly*, 10 October, XXVII (41).

AIWC (1990), *Annual Report 1989-90*, New Delhi, All India Women's Conference.

AVARD (1991), "Role of NGOs in Development: A Study of the Situation in India", New Delhi, Association of Voluntary Agencies for Rural Development (Mimeo).

BM, (1993), "Women's Development: What is the State's Intention" Bombay, *Economic and Political Weekly,* 6 March, XXVIII (10).

Bagchi, S.K. (1993), "Pipe Dream I" and "Pipe Dream II", New Delhi, *The Statesman*, 14 and 15 August.

Baviskar, Amita (1991), "The Researcher as Pilgrim", New Delhi, *Lokayan Bulletin*, 9:3/4, May-August, pp. 91-97.

Bhaskar, V. (1994), "SSP: The Environmental Impact", *The Economic Times*, 30 March.

Brown, David (1988), "Private Voluntary Organisations and Development Partnerships" in P.N. Khandwalla (ed), *Social Development: A New Role for the Organisational Sciences,* New Delhi, Sage.

Brown, David (1992), "Development Bridging Organisations and Strategic Managers for Social Change", Institute for Development Research, 9(5), May.

Brown, David and David Korten (1991), "Working Effectively with Non-governmental Organisations" in Samuel Paul and Arturo Israel (eds), *Non-Governmental Organisations and the World Bank*, Washington D.C.

Buch, M.N. (1992), "Population and Environment" in V. Gowariker (ed) *Science, Population and Development*, Pune, Unmesh Communications, pp. 86-110.

Butler, David, Ashok Lahiri and Prannoy Roy (1992), *India Decides: Elections 1952-91*, New Delhi, L M Books.

CMIE (1994), *Basic Statistics Related to Indian Economy 1993,* Bombay: Centre for Monitoring Indian Economy Pvt. Ltd.

CPR (1984), "Report on Workshop on Corporate Philanthropy", New Delhi, Ford Foundation (Mimeo)

Carroll, Thomas (1992), *Intermediary NGOs: The Supporting Link in Grassroots Development*, Kumarian Press.

Centre for Science and Environment (1982), *The State of India's Environment 1982: A Citizens's Report,* New Delhi, CSE.

Centre for Science and Environment (1985), *The State of India's Environment 1984-85: The Second Citizens' Report*, New Delhi, CSE.

Centre for Science and Environment (1991), *Floods, Flood Plains and Environment Myths*, New Delhi, CSE.

Cernea, Michael (1988), "Non-Governmental Organisations and Local Development", World Bank Discussion Paper, No. 40, Washington D.C.

Chatterjee, Meera (1990), *Indian Women: Their Health and Economic Productivity*, World Bank Discussion Paper 109.

Chitale, M.A. (1992), "Population and Water Resources of India" in V. Gowariker (ed), *Science, Population and Development*, Pune, Unmesh Communications, pp. 111-27.

Chopra, Ravi and Debashish Sen (1992), "Natural Bounty and Artificial Scarcity" in Vasant Gowariker (ed) *Science, Population and Development*, Pune, Unmesh Communications, pp. 128-60.

Covey, Jane (1992), "A Note on NGOs and Policy Influence", Institute of Development Research, September (unpublished).

Dhagamwar, Vasudha (1994), "Reflections on the Narmada Movement", New Delhi, *Seminar 413*, January.

Dighe, Anita and Sharda Jain, *Some Insights into Participatory Evaluation* : WDP.

FPAI (1992), *Annual Appraisal (1992),* Bombay, Family Planning Association of India.

Farrington, M.J. *et.al.* (eds) (1993), *Non-Governmental Organisations and the State in Asia*, London and New York, Routledge.

Gadgil, Madhav (1989), "Deforestation: Problems and Prospects", Delhi, *Lokayan Bulletin,* 7:3, May-June, pp.9-46.

Ganesh, Kamala (1993), "Gender Between family and State", Bombay, *Economic and Political Weekly*, 23 October XXVIII (43), pp. 2332-2336.

Gupta, Narendra *et.al.* (1992), "Health of Women and Children in Rajasthan", Bombay, *Economic and Politial Weekly*, 17 October XXVII (42), pp. 2323-2330.

India, Government of (1974), *Towards Equality: Report of the Committee on the Status of Women in India.* New Delhi, Government of India.

India, Government of (1988a), *shram Shakti*, Report of the National Commission on Self-Employed Women and Women in the Informal Sector, New Delhi.

India, Government of (1988b), *National Perspective for Women 1988-2000*, New Delhi; Department of Women & Child Welfare, Ministry of Human resource Development.

India, Government of (1988c), *Report of Group to Review and Simplify Procedures for Processing Proposals for Grants-in-Aid to Voluntary Agencies*, New Delhi, Ministry of Personnel, Public Grievances and Pensions.

India, Government of (1991), *Census of India, Series 1*, New Delhi.

India, Government of (1992), *Statistical Abstract: India 1990*, Central Statistical Organisation, Ministry of Planning.

India, Government of (1993), *Report 1992-93*, Ministry of Home Affairs, New Delhi.

Institute for Development Research (1992), "Development Bridging Organisations and Strategic Management for Social Change", 9(5), Boston, May.

Institute for Development Research (1992), "A Note on NGOs and Policy Influence".

Institute for Development Studies (1991), *Six Years after the Programme was Initiated: WDP; Some Emerging Challenges*, Jaipur.

Iyer, Ramaswamy R. (1993), "Not Much Headway", New Delhi, *The Hindustan Times*, 17 Nov.

Jain, Pankaj (1990), "Perspectives on Voluntary Organisation", Anand, IRMA (mimeo).

Jain, Sharda, *et al.* (1986), *Exploring Possibilities: A Review of the Women's Development Programme*, Jaipur, Rajasthan. Institute of Development Studies.

Lokayan Bulletin (1985) "Dialogues: On Threats to the Non-Party Political Process", New Delhi 3/2, April, pp. 37-49.

Kanter, Rasabeth Moss (1979), *The Measurement of Organizational Effectiveness. Productivity, Performance and Success: Issues and Dilemmas in Service and No-Profit Organisations*, Yale University, Institute for Social & Policy Studies, PONPO Working Paper No.8.

Karat, Prakash (1988), *Foreign Funding and the Philosophy of Voluntary Organisations,* New Delhi, National Book Centre.

Khan M.E. and B.C. Patel (1993), "Access to Health Care", New Delhi, *Seminar 410: Population Planning*, October.

Khanna R., N. Mehta and A. Bhatt (1991), "Voluntary Effort in Community Health", Review of the Community Health Project of SEWA-Rural. (Mimeo)

Kimberley, J.R., Miles and Associates (1980), *The Organisational Life Cycle*, San Francisco, Calif., Jossey brass.

Korten, David (1991), "The Role of Non-Governmental Organisations in Development, Changing Patterns and Perspectives" in Samuel Paul and Arturo Israel, *Non-Governmental Organisations and the World Bank*, Washington D.C.

Kothari, Rajni (1987), "Voluntary Organisations in a Plural Society", New Delhi, *The Indian Journal of Public Administration,* xxxiii (3), July-September, pp. 433-53.

Kumar, Radha (1993), *The History of Doing: An Illustrated Account of Movements for Women's Rights and Feminism in India 1800-1900*, New Delhi: Kali for Women.

Mathiasen, III, Karl (1990), "Board Passager: Three Key Stages in a Nonprofit Board's Life Cycle", NCCB Governance Series Papers, Washington, D.C., National Center for Nonprofit Boards.

Mehta, Bhavna, (1992), "Gender and Communal Riots", Bombay, *Economic and Political Weekly,* w1, XXVII (407), pp. 2522-2524.

Minhas, B.S. *et al.* (1991), "Declining Incidence of Poverty in the 1990s: Evidence versus Artefacts", Bombay6, *Economic and Political Weekly*, July 6-13.

Morse, Bradford and Thomas Berger (1992), *Sardar Sarovar: The Report of the Independent Review*, Ottawa, Resource Futures International.

Muraleedharan, T.R. (1994), "EI A: Beyond Regulation", New Delhi, *The Economic Times*, 2 March.

Oldenburg, Philip (1992), "Sex Ratio, son Preference and Violence in India" Bombay, *Economic and Political Weekly*, December 5-12, xxii (49-50) pp. 2657-2666.

Pachauri, R.K. (1992), "Population and Energy" in Vasant Gowarikar (ed.) *Science, Population and Development*, Pune, Unmesh Communications, pp. 218-43.

Pachauri, Saroj (1989), "Experiences in Community Health"; Anubhav Series, New Delhi, Parivar Seva Sanstha & Food Foundation.

Pachauri Saroj (1993), "The Problem", *Seminar 410 : Population Planning,* October.

Pai Panandiker, V.A. and Ajay K. Mehra (1987), *People's Participation in Family Planning,* New Delhi, Uppal.

Pandey, Shashi Ranjan (1991), *Community Action for Social Justice*, New Delhi, Sage.

Paul, Samuel (1989), "Poverty Alleviation and Participation: The Case for Government - Grassroots Agency Collaboration", Ford Foundation.

Phadke, Suhas (1993) "The Wastelands", Bombay, *The Independent*, 31 May.

Planning Commission (1991), *Report of the Task Force on Self-managedInstitutions for Integrated Development*, Govt. of India, December (mimeo.)

PRIA (1989), "Networks and their Functioning", New Delhi, Society for Participatory Research in Asia, September (mimeo.)

PRIA (1991), "A Study of History Roles and Future Challenges", New Delhi, Society for Participatory Research in Asia (mimeo).

Rajasthan, Government of, (1984), *Women's Development Project*, Jaipur.

Ramaswamy, Uma (1990), "Non-Government Organisations: A Perspective", Friedrich Ebert Stiftung (unpublished).

Rao, G.R.S. (1990), "Corporate Social Accountability in India", Philanthropy: Newsletter of the Centre for Advancement of Philanthropy, Bombay, Centre for Advancement of Philanthropy, 14 December, pp. 2-4.

Robinson, M.J. Farrington and S. Satish (1993), "Overview", in M.J. Farrington and D. Lewis (ed) *Non-Governmental Organisations and the State in Asia*, London and New York, Routledge.

Rose, Kalima (1992), *Where Women are Leaders : The SEWA Movement in India*, Zed Books.

SAARC (1992), *Meeting the Challenge,* Report of the Independent South Asian Commission on Poverty Alleviation, November.

Saint, Kishore (1993), "Communities and their Commons", *Seminar 406 : Our Natural Resources*, June, New Delhi, pp. 19-22.

Salamon, L.M. and Helmut Anheier (1992), "In Search of the Non-profit Sector 1: The Question of Definitions", Johns Hopkins Institute for Policy Studies, Working Paper No.2.

Satia, J.K. and S. J. Jejeebhoy (eds) (1991), *The Demographic Challenge*, New Delhi, Oxford University Press.

Sen, Jai (1986), "On Anti-Voluntarism", New Delhi, *Lokayan Bulletin*, 4(3/4), May-August, pp. 9-37.

Sen, Siddhartha (1993), *Defining the Nonprofit Sector: India,* Working Paper I, Johns Hopkins University Institute for Policy Studies.

Sharma, Suresh (1987), "voluntary Efforts and Institutional Funding", New Delhi, *Lokayan Bulletin*, 5:2.

Sheth, D.L. and Harsh Sethi (1989), "Representations and Reality: The NGO Sector".

Shiva, Vandana (1971), *Ecology and the Politics of Survival: Conflicts over Natural Resources in India,* New Delhi, Sage.

Singh, Chhatrapati (1991), *Water Rights and Principles of Water Resources Management,* under the auspices of Indian Law Institute, Bombay, N.M. Tripathi Ltd.

Singh, V.B. and Shankar Bose (1987), *State Elections in India (1952-85)*, Vols. I & II, New Delhi, Sage.

Subramanian, Ashok and Mehta, Mona (1984), A Profile of Voluntary Health Effort in Gujarat, Working Paper No. 509, Indian Institute of Management, Ahmedabad (mimeo).

Sundar, Pushpa (1994), "NGO Experience in Health: An Overview" in Saroj Pachauri (ed). *Listening to Women Talk about their Health: Issues and Evidence from India*. New Delhi, Haranand.

Tandan, Rajesh (1986), "Regulating NGOs: New Moves", New Delhi, *Lokayan Bulletin,* 4(3/4), May-August, pp. 38-43.

Tandon, Rajesh (1988), "Networks and their Functioning", Society for Participatory Research in Asia (Mimeo).

VANI (1990), "Dialogue with Donors", New Delhi, voluntary Action Network India.

Visaria Pravin, Leela Visaria and Anurdh Jain (1992), "contraceptive Use and Fertility in Gujarat", Ahmedabad, Gujarat Institute of Development Research and the Population Council, December.

World Bank (1991), *Gender and Poverty in India*, Washington D.C.

World Bank (1992), *The Women's Development Program in Rajasthan*, Washington D.C.

World Bank (1993), *World Development Report '1992'*, Oxford University Press.

APPENDIX

Indian Foundations & Trusts Providing Funds to VOs*

Andhra Pradesh

1. ANDHRA PRADESH RURAL RECONSTRUCTION MISSION (APRRM)

Address	:	1-69, Beside KBR Mills, Cross Road, Piler Chittor Distt.-517214, AP
Tel.	:	08584-244554
Contact Person	:	Mr. B. Saran Kumar

2. BYRRAJU FOUNDATION

Address	:	Satyam Enclave 2-74, Jeedimetla Village, NH-7, Secunderabad.
Tel.	:	91-40-23191725
E-mail	:	mail@byrrajufoundation.org
Web	:	www.byrrajufoundation.org
Contact person	:	Mr. B. Ramalinga Raju / P.K. Madhav
Subject Covered	:	Primary Healthcare, School Health, Eye Care, Dental Care, Epilepsy, Diabetes, Hypertension, Maternity & Child Care, Heart Disease Detection, Primary & Secondary Education, Adult Literacy, Drinking Water, Individual Sanitary Latrines, Delivery of Services.

* Source: Mainly from the *Directory of Donor Organisations*, Sampradaan Indian Centre for Philanthropy, 2005, New Delhi

3. DR. REDDY'S FOUNDATION

Address	:	6-3-668/10/77 & 78, Durganagar Colony, Punjagutta, Hyderabad-500082, Andhra Pradesh
Tel.	:	23394603/23394613, 23394607
E-mail	:	nalinig@satyam.net.in
Contact Person	:	Nalini Gangadharan

4. NAANDI FOUNDATION

Address	:	502, Trendset Towers, Road No.-2, Banjara Hills, Hyderabad-500039, Andhra Pradesh
Tel	:	91-40-55696074/75/91-40-23556491/92
E-mail	:	info@naandi.net/alina@naandi.net
Web	:	www.naandi.org
Contact Person	:	Mr. Manoj Kumar

5. SPORTS COACHING FOUNDATION

Address	:	Sports Complex, Masabtank, Hyderabad-500028
Tel	:	91-40-55522728, 9396559440
E-mail	:	sai@scfindia.org/scf_india@yahoo.com
Contact person	:	Mr. K. Sai Babu
Summary of purpose	:	To promote sports among youngsters with emphasis on cricket and tennis
Subject Covered	:	Education, Medicine and Health
Method of Activity	:	Self conducted programmes, scholarships, Children / Street Children prizes, conferences, publications.

Assam

1. RASHTRIYA GRAMIN VIKAS NIDHI

Address	:	8th Byelane, Rajgarh Road, Guwahati-781003, Assam
Tel	:	0361-2528652
E-mail	:	rgvnhol@sancharnet.in
Web	:	www.rgvindia.org
Contact person	:	Dr. Mahfuza Rahman, Executive Director
Summary of purpose	:	Income Generation Activities

Delhi

1. AMITY HUMANITY FOUNDATION

Address	: E-27, Defence Colony, New Delhi-110024
Tel	: 011-24699700/24621960
E-mail	: amitasha@akegroup.com
Web	: www.amity.edu
Contact person	: Maj. Gen. (Dr.) Surendar Kumar

2. ASHOKA FOUNDATION

Address	: T-13, Green Park Extension, New Delhi-110016
Tel	: 011-26198062/0969
E-mail	: ashokal@del3.vsnl.net.in
Contact person	: Gared Jones
Summary of purpose	: To provide support to social innovators, to promote their work and to refine their new ideas
Subject Covered	: Arts and Humanities, Rural development, Conservations & Environment, Economic Affairs, Education, Law & Human Rights, Medicine and Health, Science and Technology, STDs/AIDS Agriculture, Bio-diversity.
Method of Activity	: Publications grants to individuals, Scholarships, fellowships and training courses, Aged, Children/Street Children, Women/Sex Workers, Tribals, SC/S Ts, Other Backward Castes

3. BANARSIDAS CHANDIWALA SEWA SMARAK TRUST

Address	: Chandiwala Estate, Maa Anandmayi Marg, Kalkaji, New Delhi
Tel	: 91-11-26826201/26826202
E-mail	: sbcssts@chandiwalaestate.org
Web	: www. chandiwalaestate.org
Contact person	: Mr. Bhuwan Mohan

4. BHARATIYA YUVA SHAKTI TRUST

Address	: 23-26, Institutional Area, Lodi Road, New Delhi-110003

Tel	:	011-24693079
E-mail	:	byst.delhi@ciionline.org
Web	:	www.bystonline.org
Contact person	:	Ms. Lakshmi. V. Venkatesan

5. CHILD IN NEED INSTITUTE (CINI)

Address	:	S-II/W-113, Greater Kailash-11, New Delhi-110048
Tel	:	011-51628130
Contact person	:	Dr. K. Pappu, Deputy Director

6. CHILD RELIEF AND YOU (CRY)

Address	:	DDA Slum Wing, (Barat Ghar), Bapu Park, Kotla Mubarakpur, New Delhi-110003
Tel	:	011-24693137/4790/3159
E-mail	:	cryinfo.del@crymail.org
Web	:	www.cry.org
Contact person	:	Ms. Pervin Varma
Priority of Interest	:	Children

7. CONCERN INDIA FOUNDATION

Address	:	A-52, lst Floor, Amar Colony, Lajpat Nagar-IV, New Delhi110024
Tel	:	011-262244821/3
E-mail	:	delhi@concernindia.org
Web	:	www.concernindia.org
Contact person	:	Mr. A.B.K. Dubash, Chairman

3. DALIT FOUNDATION

Address	:	D-25/D, South Extension, Part-II, New Delhi-110049
Tel	:	011-51640929
E-mail	:	dalitfoundation@vsnl.net
Contact person	:	Mr. Santosh K. Samal

9. DR RAM MANOHAR LOHIA INTERNATIONAL TRUST

Address	:	7, Jantar Mantar Road, New Delhi-110001
Tel	:	011-23368833/98681102020
E-mail	:	javedraza@email.com
Web	:	www.drrmlinternationaltrust.org
Contact person	:	Mr. Javed Raza

10. FOUNDATION FOR SOCIAL AND HUMAN DEVELOPMENT

Address	:	1 28,11, Mohammadpur, Near Bhikaji Cama Place, New Delhi
Tel	:	011-26185053
Contact person	:	Mr. Mohad Ismail

11. FOUNDATION TO AID INDUSTRIAL RECOVERY

Address	:	No. B, Second Floor, Front Block, Sagar Apartments, 6, Tilak Marg, New Delhi-110001
E-mail	:	fairing@de12.vsnl.net.in
Contact person	:	Mr. Amarjit

12. GATES FOUNDATION

Address	:	Sanskriti Bhawan, 3rd Floor, A-10, Qutab Institutional Area, New Delhi-110016
Tel	:	011-51003100
Contact person	:	Mr. Ashok Alexander

13. GOOD EARTH EDUCATION FOUNDATION

Address	:	Common Cause House, C-5, Institutional Area, Vasant Kunj New Delhi-110070
Contact person	:	Mr. Vikram Lal, Vice-President

14. HAMDARD NATIONAL FOUNDATION

Address	:	2A/3, Asaf All Road, New Delhi-110002
Tel	:	011-23239801-04
Contact person	:	Mr. Abdul Mueed

15. HELPAGE INDIA

Address	:	C-14, Qutab Institutional Area. New Delhi-110016
Tel	:	011-5688955-59
E-mail	:	Mathew.cherian@helpageindia.org
Web	:	www.helpageindia.org
Contact person	:	Mr. Mathew Cherian, Director General
Summary of purpose	:	To work for the cause and care of disadvantaged aged persons and to improve the quality of life Method of Activity Self conducted programmes and grants to institutions, conferences, training and publications

16. I.M.C. TRUST

Address	:	A-18311, Ashok Vihar Phase-1, Delhi-110052
Tel	:	011-27254429
E-mail	:	chansun@vsnl.com
Contact person	:	Mr. S.P. Arora, Managing Trustee
Summary of purpose	:	To promote socio-economic and educational welfare of women and children from poor families
Subject Covered	:	Arts and Humanities, Education, Law & Human Rights, Medicine and Social Studies, Widows, Women; Children, Street Children, Girl Child, Orphans, Divorced Women, etc.
Method of Activity	:	Publications, self conducted programmes, grants to institutions, individuals, prizes and conferences

17. IDEAL FOUNDATION

Address	:	C-313, Majlis Park, New Delhi-110033
Tel	:	011-27675820
E-mail	:	drbhim@indiatimes.com
Contact person	:	Dr. Bhim Sam Verma

18. INDIA VISION FOUNDATION

Address	:	2, Talkatora Lane, New Delhi-110001
Tel	:	0091-11-23094814, 23094826
Fax	:	0091-11-23094761
E-mail	:	ivf@indiavisionfoundation.org / ivfindia@vsnl.com /
Web	:	www. indiavisionfoundation.org
Contact person	:	Dr. Kiran Bedi / Ms. Saina Bedi

19. INDIAN OIL FOUNDATION

Address	:	Indian Oil Corporation, Scope Complex, Core-2, Lodhi Road, New Delhi-110003
Tel	:	011-24367628
E-mail	:	kaushikmd@iocl.com / kaushikmd@yahoo.com
Contact person	:	Mr. M.D. Kaushik

20. INDUS QUALITY FOUNDATION

Address	:	Kailash Building (10th Floor), 26, K.G. Marg, New Delhi110001

Tel	:	011-23353221/331
E-mail	:	iqf@vsnl.com / iqf@iqlnet.com
Contact person	:	Mr. Debajit Das

21. K.K BIRLA FOUNDATION

Address	:	10th Floor, 18-20, Kasturba Gandhi Marg, New Delhi-110001
Tel	:	011-23317735, 23718282

22. KRISHNAMOORTHI FOUNDATION

Address	:	607, Link Apartments, 18, Mother Dairy Road, Delhi-110092
Tel	:	011-2722646
Contact person	:	Mr. R. Krishnamoorthi, Chairman
Summary of purpose	:	Economic Affairs, Human Rights, Law, Science & Technology
Method of Activity	:	Self conducted programmes and grants to others

23. LALA DIWAN CHAND TRUST

Address	:	No. 2, Jain Mandir Road, New Delhi-110001
Tel	:	011-23363536/23735747
Contact person	:	Mr. M.K. Gaur, Director
Summary of purpose	:	To provide donations to charitable societies for Needy and poor
Method of Activity	:	Grants to institutions, scholarships and fellowships

24. NATIONAL FOUNDATION FOR INDIA (NFI)

Address	:	Core-4A, Upper Ground Floor, India Habitat Centre, Lodhi Road, ND-3
Tel	:	011-24649473/23641864/5
E-mail	:	ajay_s_mehta@nfi.org.in
Contact person	:	Mr. Ajay S. Mehta, Executive Director

25. PHD RURAL DEVELOPMENT FOUNDATION

Address	:	PHD House, Opp. Asian Games Vill., New Delhi-110016
Tel	:	011-26561443, 26863801-04
E-mail	:	phdcci@phdecimail.coin
Web	:	www.phdcci.org
Contact person	:	Mr. Teevra Sharma

26. POPULATION FOUNDATION OF INDIA

Address	:	B-28, Qutab Institutional Area, Tara Crescent, New Delhi110016
Tel	:	91-11-26867080/26867081/26523741
E-mail	:	popfound@sify.com
Web	:	www.popfound.org
Contact person	:	Mr. A.R. Nanda, Executive Director

27. PRICONSER (INDIA)

Address	:	607, Link House, 18, Mother Dairy Road, Delhi-110092
Tel	:	011-2722646
Contact person	:	Mr. R. Krishnamoorthi
Summary of purpose	:	Technology development, Systems design, Mass communication
Subject Covered	:	Conservation and the Environment, International Affairs, Social Welfare and Social Studies, Economically Weaker Sections

28. RAI BAHADUR GUJARMAL MODI FOUNDATION

Address	:	Modicare, 4, Community Centre, New Friends Colony, New Delhi-110065
Tel	:	91-11-26321441-50 Extn. 303,231, 304
E-mail	:	support@modicare.com
Web	:	www.modicare.com
Contact person	:	Mr. Samir Modi

29. RAJIV GANDHI FOUNDATION

Address	:	Jawahar Bhawan; Dr. Rajendra Prasad Road, New Delhi110001
Tel	:	011-23755117/118
E-mail	:	info@rgfindia.com
Web	:	www.rgfindia.com
Contact person	:	Mr. M. Malhoutra, Secretary General

30. RAMJAS FOUNDATION

Address	:	4609, Ansari Road, Daryaganj, New Delhi-110002
Tel	:	011-23271226/23263284
Contact person	:	Shri Ram Kanwar Gupta

31. RAUNAQ EDUCATION FOUNDATION

Address	: Raunaq Singh c/o BST Ltd., Allahabad Bank Building, 17, Parliament Street, New Delhi-110001

32. ROTARY CLUB OF DELHI CITY

Address	: A-1 /49, Safdarjang Enciave, New Delhi-110029
Tel	: 011-26863018/26854859
Contact person	: Mr. Ramesh Aggarwal
Summary of purpose	: To promote the cause of philanthropy
Subject Covered	: Arts and Humanities, Conservation and the Environment, Education, Medicine and Health, Social Welfare and Social Studies, AIDS, Aged, Children/Street Children
Method of Activity	: Self conducted programmes, grants to institutions and scholarships, fellowships, prizes, conference and training courses

33. ROTARY EDUCATION FOUNDATION RI. DISTRICT 3010

Address	: 2750, Sharan Kutir, Kashmere Gate. New Delhi-110006
Tel	: 011-23964064
Contact person	: Mr. Vimal K. Gupta
Summary of purpose	: To help children from poor families to pursue higher studies in engineering; medicine and architecture Subject Covered Education, Medicine and Health, Science and Technology, Research, architecture and engineering
Method of Activity	: Self conducted programmes, Scholarships, Fellowships and prizes for Needy students, destitutes & physically handicapped

34. SAMUEL FOUNDATION CHARITABLE TRUST

Address	: 1st Floor, MCD Community Centre, B-Block Market, Tagore Garden, New Delhi-110027
Tel	: 011-25454021

E-mail	:	samuelfoundation@sify.com
Contact person	:	Ms. Arpna Luthra

35. SANSKRITI FOUNDATION

Address	:	C-11, Qutab Institutional Area, New Delhi-110016
Tel	:	011-26527677/26963220
E-mail	:	opjain@sanskritifoundation.org
Web	:	www.sanskritifoundation.org
Contact person	:	Mr. O.P. Jain

36. SHIVAM FOUNDATION

Address	:	F-5, Okhla Industrial Area, Phase-1, New Delhi-110020
Tel	:	011-26813586
Contact person	:	Mr. T.K. Ganju

37. SHRI GOPAL CHANDRA TRUST

Address	:	3/13-B, Asaf Ali Road, New Delhi-110002
Tel	:	011-23275761
Contact person	:	Mr. S.K. Aggarwal

38. SHRIRAM WASHESHRAN DEVI BHATIA MEMORIAL CHARITABLE TRUST

Address	:	C-378, Defence Colony, New Delhi-110024
Tel	:	011-24692125
Contact person	:	Dr. J.M. Bhatia
Summary of purpose	:	To give recognition and awards in the field of social work
Subject Covered	:	Rural Development, Conservation and the Environment, Education, Law & Human Rights, Medicine and Ilealth, Science and Technology, Social Welfare and Social Studies
Method of Activity	:	Grants to institutions and individuals, scholarships, fellowships, prizes, sponsorship of eye and blood donation camps, awards in the field of social work
Priority of Interest	:	Aged, Children, Street Children, Women and Sex Workers
Further Information	:	Notified through press/normally 30th Oct.

39. SMITA PATIL FOUNDATION

Address	:	Chemon Estate, Babu Jagjiwan Ram Marg, Behind D-4, Vasant Kuni, New Delhi-110070
Tel	:	011-26896056
E-mail	:	smita_foundation@vsnl.net
Contact person	:	Ms. Manya Patii

40. SOCIAL DEVELOPMENT FOUNDATION

Address	:	188, Master Block, Delhi-110092
Tel	:	011-22462528
E-mail	:	vbrawat@vsnl.com
Web	:	www.thesdf.org
Summary of purpose	:	To impart scientific education and temperament among the masses.Use rationalists traditions and methods in the Developmental sector
Method of Activity	:	Providing legal aid to victims of violence on the marginalized sections of society particularly women, Networking of the grassroot organizations working for the development of tribals, Dalits and backward classes of the minorities

41. THE CORBETT FOUNDATION

Address	:	405, International Trade Tower, Nehlu Place, New Delhi-110019
Tel	:	011-51608505
E-mail	:	Corbett_foundation@yahoo.com
Web	:	www.corbettfoundation.org

42. THE INDUSIND FOUNDATION

Address	:	193, Rouse Avenue, New Delhi-110002
Tel	:	011-23235680
Contact person	:	Mr. A.C. Asram

43. THE INLAKS FOUNDATION

Address	:	St. Stephen's College, University of Delhi. Delhi-110007
E-mail	:	inlaks@del2.vsnl.net.in
Web	:	www.inlaksfoundation.org
Contact person	:	Dr. Vibha S. Chauhan

44. THE LOOMBA TRUST

Address	:	Suite No. 13-14, 31, Prithviraj Road, New Delhi-110011
Tel	:	91-11-24636832
E-mail	:	faisal@theloombatrust.org
Web	:	www.theloombatrust.org
Contact person	:	Mr. S.K. Khanna, Trustee
Summary of purpose	:	To educate children of poor widows in India
Subject Covered	:	Education
Method of Activity	:	Self conducted programmes, grants to individuals, scholarships
Priority of Interest	:	Children/Street Children

45. TIMES FOUNDATION

Address	:	7, Bahadurshah Shah Zafar Marg, New Delhi-110002
Tel	:	011-23302864/23302103
E-mail	:	timesfoundation@timesgroup.com
Web	:	www.timesfoundation.indiatimes.com
Contact person	:	Mr Pooran Chandra Pandey

46. UNNITI FOUNDATION

Address	:	140, 2nd Floor, Sunder Nagar, New Delhi-110003
Tel	:	011-24651901
E-mail	:	unniti@vsnl.com
Contact person	:	Mr. Kaval Gulhati

47. VIJAYA GUJRAL FOUNDATION

Address	:	18, Kautilya Marg, Chanakyapuri, New Delhi-110001
Tel	:	011-26872789
E-mail	:	vvgujral@hotmail.com / guira118@ndb.vsnl.net.in
Contact person	:	Dr. V.V. Gujral

48. VIKRAM SARABHAI FOUNDATION

Address	:	Core-4A, 5'h Floor, Lodhi Road, India Habitat Centre, New Delhi-110003
Tel	:	011-24643110
Contact person	:	Mr. Sudhir Kakar

49. VINOD DIKSHIT FOUNDATION

Address	:	AB-17, Mathura Road. New Delhi-110001
Tel	:	011-23071212/23071313
Contact person	:	Mrs. Sheila Dikshit

50. VISION FOUNDATION

Address	:	207/12, Prakash Mohall, East of Kailash, New Delhi-110065
Tel	:	011-26434214
E-mail	:	vision_consulting@vsnl.com
Contact person	:	Prof. S. Ranjan Mohapatra

51. WORLD ENVIRONMENT FOUNDATION

Address	:	M-64, Greater Kailash-11, New Delhi-110048
Tel	:	011-51636294, 51636716/17, 9811135151
E-mail	:	iod@vsnl.com
Web	:	www.wef.ore.uk
Summary of purpose	:	WEF is engaged in sustainable livelihood, alleviate poverty & reduce inequalities. It also organizes specific training programmes, events, workshops, conferences and seminars round the year to sensitize Corporations and Communities to improve the quality of environment.

52. ZAKAT FOUNDATION

Address	:	7, Bahadurshah Shah Zafar Marg, New Delhi-110025
Tel	:	011-26327031/26982781
E-mail	:	info@godsgraocs.org
Contact person	:	Dr. S. Zafar Mahamood, President
Summary of purpose	:	Charity
Subject Covered	:	Orphans, widows. patients, students and poor girls (marriage)

53. AGA KHAN FOUNDATION

Address	:	Sarojini House, 2nd Floor, 6, Bhagwan Das Road, New Delhi110001
Tel	:	011-23782173/57 Extn.-35

E-mail	:	general@.akfindia.org
Web	:	www.akdn.org/india
Contact person	:	Mr. Nicolas Mekinsley, Director

Gujarat

1. AHMEDABAD COMMUNITY FOUNDATION

Address	:	E-3, Vishrut Apartment, Next to A-One School, Near Subhash Chowk, Memnagar, Ahmedabad-380052, Gujarat
Tel	:	91-79-7498687, 7496657
E-mail	:	info@acfindia.org
Web	:	www.acfindia.org
Contact person	:	Ms. Bhavna Ramrakhiani

2. AMBER ASHRAYE MANILA BENEFIT ASSOCIATION

Address	:	"Hari Om". Samanvay Chowk, Jayant Society, Mavdi Plot, Rajkot-360004, Gujarat
E-mail	:	ambarajkot@yahoo.com
Contact person	:	Mr. Balvantbhai Desai

3. DEEPAK CHARITABLE FOUNDATION

Address	:	9/10, Kunj Society, Alka Puri, Baroda, Baroda-390007, Gujarat Tel 23514439,12359410
E-mail	:	arunalakhani@rediffnnail.com
Contact person	:	Mrs. Aruna Lakham
Summary of purpose	:	Running own project with hospital facility for Leprosy/ "1 'B control.Providing grants for NGOs working in the field of Leprosy/TB control. Establishment of reconstructive surgical unit in the projects.. Establishment of Technical support teams at District level for the Government Public structure in Leprosy and TB control programmes.
Priority of Interest	:	Leprosy/TB Patients. District health facilities

4. DR J.M. DESAI EDUCATIONAL CHARITABLE TRUST

Address	:	A - Omnagar, Mavdi Plot, Behind Patel Bording, Rajkot, Gujarat

Contact person : Shri Dilipbhai Desai

5. GRAMYA VIKAS TRUST

Address : Okhla Highway Road, Opp. S.T. Bus Station, Dwarka-361335, Gujarat

Tel : 02892-236551/52

E-mail : gvtdwarka@yahoo.com

Contact person : Prof D.S. Ker

6. HARKASHI EDUCATION TRUST

Address : SAI', A-1, Ashruta Park.. Near Vijay Nagar, Harni Road. Baroda.

Tel : 2488088

Contact person : Mr. Jyotish Kumar Solanki

7. INDIAN HEART FOUNDATION & RESEARCH INSTITUTE

Address : C-11, Silver Are. Near Gujarat Railway Crossing, Ellisbridge, Ahmedabad-380006, Gujarat

Tel : 26445445, 26444101

Contact person : Dr. Nitin Shah

Summary of purpose : To provide medical services, health education, rehabilitation services and medical research.

Subject Covered : Rural Development, Education, Medicine and Health, Science and Technology, Research

Method of Activity : Grants to institutions and individuals

Priority of Interest : Children, Women

8. KALP DARSH FOUNDATION TRUST

Address : "Kamala" Dinkar Colony, Jayant K.G. Road, Rajkot -360004

Tel : 2360472

Contact person : Mr. A.J. Bhatt

9. LALBHAI DALPATBHAI TRUST

Address : 1st Floor, Akshay, 53, Shrunati Society, Navrangpura, Ahmedabad-380009

Tel : 079-407454

Contact person : The Executive Director

10. LOK KALYAN TRUST (NAVJEEVAN WELFARE CENTRE)

Address : Lodhika, Rajkot -360035, Gujarat

Tel : 02827-44338

Contact person : Mr. Roy. Pazmampillil

11. LOK SEVAK MANDAL

Address : Servants of the People Society, Lajpat Bhavan, Harni Road. Vadodara.

Tel : 2488757/2482807

Fax : 0265-2488757

Contact person : Mr. Manubhai Patel

12. MAHARAJA SHRI LAKHDHIRAJ1 ENDOWMENT TRUST

Address : V.C. Park, Anath Ashram Building, Near Patel Boarding, Morbi-363641, Distt. Rajkot, Gujarat

Tel : 02822-222284

Contact person : Dr. Ambrishbhai S. Bhatt

13. MANAV KALYAN TRUST

Address : 10, Swastik Super Market, 4th Floor, Opp. Popular House, Ashram Road, Ahmedabad-380009, Gujarat

Tel : 079-6580361

E-mail : psavitri13@yahoo.com

Contact person : Ms. Savitri Patel

14. NATIONAL INNOVATION FOUNDATION

Address : B-4, Ravi Niketan, Nehru Park, Vastrapur, Ahmedabad-380015

Tel : 91-79-26732456/2095

E-mail : info@nifindia.org

Web : www.nifindia.org

Summary of purpose : To ensure evolution and diffusion of green grassroots innovations in a time bound and mission oriented manner. To support sustaining and scaling up of grassroots green innovations and link innovation, enterprises and investments. To create a Knowledge Network. To promote possible commercial and noncommercial applications of innovations and incorporate it in education curriculum, development programmes and policies.

15. NAVINCHANDRA MAFATLAL SADGURU WATER AND DEVELOPMENT FOUNDATION

Address	:	Post Box No.-71, Dahod-389151, Gujarat
Tel	:	0091-2673-238601/238602
Contact person	:	Mr. Hamath Jagawat, Managing Trustee and Director
Summary of purpose	:	Integrated rural development, natural resource management, small scale water resources development, joint-forest management, formation of village institutions around economic initiatives
Subject Covered	:	Rural & tribal people, environment, health, socio-economic Development; training for strengthening of village institutions, training in natural resource management
Priority of Interest	:	Rural and Tribal people

16. SHREE MURLIDHAR KHADI GRAM UDHYOG SEVA TRUST

Address	:	3, New Vishwanagar, R.M.C. Qtr. No. 15/2152, 56 - Feet Road, Mavdiplot, Rajkot, Gujarat
Tel	:	9825259466 (Mobile)
Contact person	:	Mr. Rameshbhai R. Rathod

17. SMT. NATHIBA HARGOVINDAS LAXMICHAND CHARITABLE TRUST

Address	:	2nd Floor, P.K. House, Ellisbridge, Ahmedabad-380006, Gujarat
Tel	:	079-6578782
Contact person	:	Mrs. Priti Amit Sheth
Summary of purpose	:	To alleviate poverty by helping the needy
Subject Covered	:	Education, Medicine and Health, Social Welfare and Social Studies
Method of Activity	:	Grants to institutions and individuals, scholarships, fellowships and prizes
Priority of Interest	:	Economically disadvantaged

18. SWARODAY TRUST

Address	:	3, Jaybee Apartment, 1 Collegewadi, Near Kotak School, Rajkot -360001, Gujarat
Tel	:	0281-2695294./2695303/ 09825076499 (M)

E-mail : technicare@icenet. net
Contact person : Mr. Balendra Vaghela

Haryana

1. CH. BANSI LAL MEMORIAL TRUST
Address : Vijay Nagar Colony, Bhiwani-127021, Haryana
Tel : 9810546802
Contact person : Mr. Anirudh Chaudhary
Subject Covered : Health, Women & Child Development, Education, Beneficial Services in rural areas, Upliftment of economically weaker sections, Art & Culture
2. LALA SOHANLAL JAGMOHAN LAL KHANNA EDUCATIONAL AND CHARITABLE TRUST
Address : 960, Sector-14, Faridabad-121007, Haryana
Tel : 283296
Contact person : Mr. Kewal Krishan Khanna
Summary of purpose : To provide assistance for vocational and technical education
Subject Covered : Rural Development, Education, Social Welfare and Social Studies
Method of Activity : Self conducted programmes, Grants to individuals, institutes, scholarships and fellowships
3. RANBAXY SCIENCE FOUNDATION
Address : 20, Sector-18, Udyog Vihar, Institutional Area, Gurgaon-122001, Haryana
Tel : 95124-2342001
E-mail : omprakash.sood@ranbaxy.com
Web : www.ranbaxy.com baxyseiencefoundation.htm
Contact person : Dr. O.P. Sood
4. SNS FOUNDATION
Address : 88-89, Industrial Development Colony, Mehrauli-Gurgaon Road, Gurgaon-122001, Haryana

Tel : 0124-2333851, 2333129,2307258, 2321665
E-mail : info@snsf.org
Web : www.snsf.org
Contact person : Ms. Indira Varadarajan
Subject Covered : Health, Education, Natural Resource Management Sustainable Livelihood. Governance and Social Justice

5. S.M. SEHGAL FOUNDATION
Address : 289, Sector-17A, Gurgaon-122001, Haryana
Tel : 95124-2397621/22/5010426
E-mail : smsf@smsfoundation.org
Web : www.smsfoundation.org
Contact person : Dr. Ellora Mubhashir
Summary of purpose : Sehgal Foundation is both a funding and an implementing organization. The organizations they fund are partnerships to leverage the resources of the Foundation and those of others. This approach is part of the Foundation's commitment to pool strengths, learn from others and work with them to the best benefit of the villagers in need.
Subject Covered : Must pertain to Rural India.

Jharkhand

1. MOHMADIA EDUCATION DEVELOPMENT CENTRE
Address : ViP-Parsani, P.O.-Kanki, P.S.-Poiojari, Distt-Deoghar, Jharkhand- 815332
Tel : 252034
Contact person : Md. Nazrul Ansari, Secretary
Summary of purpose : To establish, run or manage educational centre, to take health related problem, safe drinking water, social evils, arts & music, rural games & sports, food & nutrition
Subject Covered : Arts and Humanities, Education, Medicine and Health, Social Welfare and Social Studies

Method of Activity : Grants to others, Grant Making to institutions and Grants to individuals

Priority of Interest : Children, Street Children, Women Aved/SC/STs and Other Backward Castes.

2. PROTON CHARITABLE TRUST

Address : C/o. Computer Media (India) Consultants Pvt. Ltd., Shanti Bhawan.

Bank More, Dhanbad, Jharkhand

Tel : 6326-2302112

E-mail : cmic@vsnl.com

Contact person : Mr. R.R. Srivastva

Karnataka

1. AGRICULTUTRAL DEVELOPMENT AND TRANING SOCIETY (ADATS)

Address : 10, 2nd Cross, Shanthivana, Sahakarnagar Post, Bangalore560092

Web : www.adats.com

Contact person : Mr. Ram Esteves

Summary of purpose : To unify the poor and build the structures and discipline of the Coolie Sangha at the Village, Cluster and Taluk levels.

2. AMICI DI RAOUL FOLLFREAU TRUST (AIFU)

Address : No. 58, 4th Cross, Kaveri Layout, Thavarekere Main Road, Dharmaram College post, Bangalore-560029, Karnataka

Tel : 086-51106291/255311264

E-mail : aifo@aifoindia.org

Web : www.aifoindia.org

Contact person : Mr. Jose M.V. Administrator

Summary of purpose : Eradication of Leprosy

Subject Covered : Education and Medicine and health

Method of Activity : Grants to others

Priority of Interest : Disabled persons and vulnerable children

3. ASHWINI CHARITABLE TRUST

Address	:	2-D, Kenilworth Apartments, 6, Gangadhar Chetty Road, Ulsoor, Bangaiore-560642, Karnataka
Tel	:	080-5599258
Contact person	:	Ms. Sujata Mukherjee

3. AZIM PREMJI FOUNDATION

Address	:	5, Papanna Street, St. Mark's Road Cross, Bangalore-560001.
Tel	:	080-22274404/3665/2264
E-mail	:	info@azimpremjifoundation.co.in
Web	:	www.azimpremjifoundation.org
Contact person	:	Shubhra Jvotsna, Member - Advocacy and Communication
Subject Covered	:	Education'economic backwardness of the area High number of school children High number of school girl children Poor learning levels

4. CHRISTEL HOUSE INDIA

Address	:	Yelahanka Main Road, Kannur Post via Bagalur, Bangalore East
Tel	:	91-080-56979133,56979144
E-mail	:	christelhouse@vsnl.org
Web	:	www.christelhouseindia.org
Contact person	:	Ms. Parvathi Nair
Summary of purpose	:	To help children around the world break the cycle of Poverty.

5. FREEDOM FOUNDATION

Address	:	180, Hennur Cross, Bangalore -560043, Karnataka
Tel	:	080-25440134, 25440135, 25443101
E-mail	:	freedom@bgl.vsnl.net.in
Web	:	www.thefreedomfoundation.org
Contact person	:	Mr. Ashok K. Rau

6. INFOSYS FOUNDATION

Address	:	III Floor, Infosys Towers, Bannerghatta Road, Bangalore - 560076
Tel	:	91-80-26588668

Fax	:	91-80-26588676
E-mail	:	foundation@infy.com / srinivasrao@infy.com
Web	:	www.infosysfoundation.org
Contact person	:	Ms. Sudha Murty

7. STELLA MARY'S WOMEN WELFARE ASSOCIATION

Address	:	Near Municipal High School, Chitwadigi Hospet, Bellary Distt., Karnataka
Tel	:	08394-424304
E-mail	:	smwwa@hpt.yahoo.com
Contact person	:	Ms. Mini Mathew

8. VIVEKANANDA FOUNDATION

Address	:	54, "Vidya", Paramhamsa Road; Yadavagiri, Mysore-570020, Karnataka
Tel	:	(821) 513366/514000
Contact person	:	Dr. R. Balasubramanium, President
Summary of purpose	:	To establish a network of organizations and individuals who have started service activities insuired by the ideals of Swami Vivekananda
Subject Covered	:	Education, Medicine and Health, Social Welfare and Social tudies, Rural Development and Human Resource Development
Method of Activity	:	Self-conducted programmes and grants to others
Priority of Interest	:	Children, Street Children, Women, Tribals and SC/STs

Maharashtra

1. A.H. WADIA CHARITABLE TRUST

Address	:	Temple Bar Building, 70, Dr. V.B. Gandhi Road, Mumbai400023

2. ALKESH DINESH MODI MEMORIAL TRUST

Address	:	924, Stock Exchange Tower, Dalal Street, Fort, Mumbai-400023
Tel	:	022-22723617-18
E-mail	:	dineshbhaimody@rediff.com

Contact person : Mr. Dinesh Mody, Chairman
Subject Covered : Spiritual, Medical, Education, Poor
Method of Activity : Grant making to institutions, Prizes and conferences
Priority of Interest : Poor

3. AMBUJA CEMENT FOUNDATION
Address : C/o, Gujarath Ambuia Cement Ltd., C.S.T. Road, Near Vidyanagari, Kalina, Santacruz (E), Mumbai-400098, Maharashtra
Tel : 022-56931800 / 18
E-mail : cdekal@ambujamail.com
Web : www.acf.org
Contact person : Ms. Peari Tiwari, General Manager
Summary of purpose : To energise, involve and enable communities to realize their potential.

4. AMIT PANDYA PUBLIC CHARITABLE TRUST
Address : 1202/B, Park Side-2, Raheja Estate. Road No. 1, Borivli (E), Mumbai
Contact person : Mr. V.H. Pandya

5. ANAND ASHRAM TRUST
Address : 1st Floor, Industry House, Near Aakashvam Bhavan, 159 Churchgate
Reclamation, Mumbai-400020, Maharashtra
Tel : 022-22029505
E-mail : sandeep_mahajan@cheguemail.com
Contact person : Mr. Sandeep Mahajan

6. ANARDE FOUNDATION
Address : 409. New 1Jdyog Mandir No. 2, Moghul Lane, Mahim West, Mumbai
Tel : 91-22-24469341/24456967
E-mail : anardefoundation@vsnl.net / anardefoundation@hathway.com
Contact person : Mrs. Margarida Crasto, Sr. Manager HRD and Admin
Summary of purpose : To work for Poverty Alleviation, Women Empowement & Child Welfare, to provide education & training and to increase social & cultural awareness.

7. ANJUMAN-UL-KHARUL ISLAM

Address	:	92, D.N. Road, C. ST. Fort, Near TOI, Mumbai-400 001, Maharashtra
Tel	:	022-2620177
Fax	:	022-2621610
E-mail	:	aiaims@bom4vsnl.net.in
Contact person	:	Dr. Ishaq Jamkhanwala
Subject Covered	:	Education, Social Welfare and Social Studies
Method of Activity	:	Scholarships, fellowships and training courses
Priority of Interest	:	Widows, Women, Children, and Street Children

8. ASIAN PAINTS CHARITABLE TRUST

Address	:	5th Floor, Nirmal, Nariman Point, Mumbai-400021, Maharashtra
Tel	:	022-22024544
Fax	:	022-22028993
Contact person	:	Mr. R.D. Dam
Subject Covered	:	Education, medicine and health

9. BAI HILLA RUSTOMJI BUHARIWALA CHARITY TRUST

Address	:	C/o R.N. Rustomji Co, Srinivas House, H. Somani Road, Mumbai

10. BAI RATANBAI & SETH JEHANGIR PARDIWALA CHARITY TRUST

Address	:	Dubash Mansion, Walton Road, Near Electric House, Colaba, Mumbai
Tel	:	022-22840893
Contact person	:	Capt. H.J.M. Desai, Managing Trustee
Summary of purpose	:	The Trust deed permits assistance only to Parsi Zorastrians for education, medical assistance, relief of poverty, relief to disabled and to institutions for Zorastrians promoting above objectives.
Subject Covered	:	Research especially into Ayurvedic practices
Method of Activity	:	Research

11. BOMBAY COMMUNITY PUBLIC TRUST

Address	:	Earnest House, 7th Floor, Nariman Point, Mumbai-400021

Tel : 022-2845928/2836672
E-mail : bcpt@vsul.com
Web : www.bcpt.org.in
Contact person : Ms. Harsha Parekh

12. CHHATLOK POONAM FOUNDATION

Address : 280, L.T. Marg, Ramchandra Bldg., Mumbai-400002
Tel : 2080351/2083278

13. CHILD RELIEF AND YOU (CRY)

Address : 189-A, Anand Estate, Sane Guruji Marg, Mumbai-400011
Tel : 0091-022-23096845/23063651/3647
E-mail : cryinfo.mum@ crymail.org
Summary of purpose : To support initiatives centred on the development of underprivileged children, empowerment of mothers, women, community development and income generation activities.
Subject Covered : Education, Medicine and Health, Social Welfare and Social Studies, Research. Fundraising, Awareness Raising
Method of Activity : Grants to institutions and individuals, scholarships, fellowships, training courses and publications
Priority of Interest : Children, Street Children, Women, tribal children, SC/ST children, bonded labourers, child labour, children of prostitutes, children of undertrials & orphans

14. CONCERN INDIA FOUNDATION

Address : 3rd Floor, Ador House, 6-K, Dubash Marg, Mumbai-400001
Tel : 2855487
E-mail : concern@bom4.vsnl.net.in
Contact person : Mrs. Kavita Shah, Chief Executive Officer
Summary of purpose : Development through participation
Subject Covered : Rural Development, Conservation and the Environment, Education, Health, Social Welfare and Community Organisation

Method of Activity : Grants to institutions
Priority of Interest : Aged, Children/Women/Sex Workers, Tribals, Handicapped

15. D.H. BAKHRU FOUNDATION
Address : Bldg No.9, Flat No.602, Mazda HIG Complex, Oshiwara, Andheri (W), Mumbai-400053
Tel : 022-26398779/26398825
E-mail : hkbakhru@hotmail.com
Contact person : Mr. Ramesh Bakhru

16. DHIRUBHAI AMBANI FOUNDATION
Address : 4th Floor, Court House, L.T. Marg, Dhobi Talab, Mumbai400002
Tel : 022-22088134
Contact person : Mr. Arun Bhende

17. DINSHAW JAMESHEDJI BAHADURJI CHARITIES
Address : C/o. Mazda Chemicals, 97, Bhiwandi Hsg. Soc 97, August Kranti Marg, Cumballa Hill Hospital, Mumbai-400026

18. DIWALIBEN MOHANLAL MEHTA CHARITABLE TRUST
Address : Khatau Mansion, 1st Floor, Oomer Park, 95-K, Bhulabhai Desai Road, Mumbai-400036
Tel : 022-23691334/23632866/23633082/23648919
E-mail : diwalibn@bom5vsnl.net.in
Contact person : Shri Mafatlal M. Mehta

19. ELAVIA TRUST
Address : C/o. Ms. Perin Jehangir, Jupiter Bldg., 27th Floor, Cuffe Parade, Mumbai-400005, Maharashtra
Tel : 22184779, 22185822

20. FAIR & LOVELY FOUNDATION
Address : P.O. Box No.11281, Marine I,mes Post Office, Mumbai-400002 Maharashtra
Contact person : Director

21. FAMILY WELFARE TRUST
Address : Opp. Holy Family School, S.B. Road, Colaba, Mumbai-400005

Tel	:	3082085
Subject Covered	:	Medicine and Health
Method of Activity	:	Grants to institutions and individuals
Priority of Interest	:	Needy and poor patients

22. FRAMJI PESTONJI DIVECHA CHARITY TRUST

Address	:	C/o. Rear Admiral H.D. Kapadia (Managing Trustee), 161, Silver Arch, 66, Nepean Sea Road, Mumbai-400006

23. FRENY SHIAWA MISTRY EDUCATION TRUST

Address	:	Freny Shiawa Mistry Education Trust, Maharishi Karve Road, Mumbai-400001

24. G.D. BIRLA MEDICAL RESEARCH AND EDUCATION FOUNDATION

Address	:	91/92, Sahkar Bhavan, 23, Nariman Point, Mumbai-400021
Tel	:	2029505
E-mail	:	sandeep mahajan@chequemail.com
Contact person	:	Mr. Sandeep Mahajan, Officer on Special Duty
Summary of purpose	:	Donate aid to needy, poor patients
Subject Covered	:	Arts and Humanities, Conservation and the Environment, Education, Medicine and Health, Science and Technology, Social Welfare and Social Studies, Research and Sports
Method of Activity	:	Self conducted programmes and grants to others. Institutions and Individuals, scholarships and fellowships etc., conferences and publications
Priority of Interest	:	Economically weaker sections and under privileged

25. GOODLAS NEROLAC PAINTS CHARITABLE TRUST

Address	:	Ganpat Rao Kadam Marg, P.O. Box No. 16322, L. Parel, Mumbai-400013
Contact person	:	Director

26. HABITAT FOR HUMANITY

Address	:	22/6, Ishwar Bhawan, A Road Churchgate, Mumbai-400020
Tel	:	22049815/23082157
Contact person	:	Secretary

27. HINDUJA FOUNDATION

Address	:	Hinduja House, 171, Dr. Annie Besant Road, Worli, Mumbai400018
Tel	:	022-24960707
Web	:	www.hindujagroup.com / hindujafoundation.htm
Contact person	:	President
Summary of purpose	:	Establish and maintain hospital and provide healthcare to the poor, to establish and support educational institutions, grant scholarships & encourage excellence in education in other ways, to fund social welfare activities, to promote relief in the event of natural calamities
Subject Covered	:	Arts and Humanities, Conservation and Environment, Education, Medicine and Health, Science and Technology, Social Welfare and Social Studies, Research and Sports
Method of Activity	:	Research

28. HOMAI DORABJI CHOKSI TRUST

Address	:	B-1, Eden Hall, Dr. Annie Besant Road, Worli, Mumbai-400018

29. HORMASJEE D. KAPADIA TRUST FUND

Address	:	C/o. Crawford Bailley, State Bank Bldg,, Bank Street, Mumbai-400023
Tel	:	022-22663713

30. IRANIAN ZOROASTRIAN ANJUMAN

Address	:	Kermani Bldg., 2nd Floor; P.M. Road, Mumbai-400001
Tel	:	022-22040401

31. J.A. WADIA CHARITABLE TRUST

Address	:	89, Nepean Sea Road, Mumbai-400006

32. J.N. TATA ENDOWMENT

Address	:	Mulla House, 4th Floor, 51, M.G. Road, Mumbai-400001

33. JAGRUTI TRUST

Address	:	C/o. Mr. A.S. Bhatena, Chairman, 6-A, Boat Club Road, Pune411001

34. JAMNALAL BAJAJ FOUNDATION

Address	:	Bajaj Bhawan, 2nd Floor, 226, Nariman Point, Jamnalal Bajaj Marg, Mumbai-400021
Tel	:	022-2023626
Contact person	:	Dr. L.M. Singhvi

35. JAMSHED AND SHIRIN GUZDAR TRUST

Address	:	Neville House, Ballard Estate, Mumbai-400001

36. JEEJEEBHOY CHARITIES

Address	:	2nd Floor, Mangalore Street, Ballard Estate, Mumbai-400038
Contact person	:	J.A. Dhondy

37. J.V. GOKAL CHARITY TRUST

Address	:	Kasturi Building, 2nd Floor, 171/172, Jamshedji Tata Road, Mumbai-400020

38. K.C. MAHINDRA EDUCATION TRUST

Address	:	Mahindra & Mahindra Limited, Gateway Building, Stevens Street, Apollo Bunder, Mumbai-400001
Tel	:	022-2021031
Contact person	:	Mr. S. Ganapathy

39. KATGARA FUND

Address	:	C/o. Jeena & Co., Elephinstone Bldg., 10, Veer Nariman Road, Stevens Street, Fort Mumbai-400001
Tel	:	22042032

40. KERAWALA CHARITY TRUST

Address	:	C/o. Dr. A.S. Irani, Kerawala Mansion, Carnae Road, Mumbai400023

41. KHURSHED & TEHMURASP MULLA TRUST

Address	:	C/o. Mr. M.N. Mulla, Jehangir Wadia Bldg., 51, M.G. Road, Muinbai-400023

42. KOTAK FOUNDATION

Address	:	Kotak & Co., Navsari Bldg., D.N. Road; Mumbai

43. KRISHNA KAMAL CHARITY TRUST

Address	:	507, Raheja Centre, 214, Nariman Point, Mumbai-400021
Tel	:	022-22844428

Contact person	:	Mr. S.K. Khaitan

44. KUNWARHARI SINGLAL SINGH TRUST

Address	:	5, Heera Building, Tilak Road, Mumbai-400002
Tel	:	2081599

45. LALA LAJPAT RAI MEMORIAL TRUST

Address	:	Lala Lajpat Rai Marg, Haji Ali, Mumbai-400034
Tel	:	24928240/24928241
Web	:	www.llim.edu
Contact person	:	Mr. M.G. Shrihatti
Summary of purpose	:	To promote education
Method of Activity	:	Education, Research, Grant making to institutions, Training to students for higher study and Publications
Priority of Interest	:	Backward Castes
Further Information	:	30th Sept. every year

46. LIFE-LET INDIVIDUALS FEEL

Address	:	4, Samadhan, Linking Road Extension, Santa Cruz(W), Mumbai-400050
Tel	:	26146958
Contact person	:	President

47. LION'S CLUB OF MUMBAI, BYCULLA

Address	:	5, Khururu Baugh, S.B. Road. Colaba, Mumbai-400005
Tel	:	022-2049131
Contact person	:	Mr. Bepsi Daruwala

48. MAHINDRA FOUNDATION

Address	:	Cecil Court, 3rd Floor, Next to Regal Cinema, Colaba, Mumbai 400039
Tel	:	022-22021031
Contact person	:	Mr. P.K. Patil
Subject Covered	:	Rural Development, Conservation and Environment, Education, Medicine and Health

49. MAKE-A-WISH FOUNDATION

Address	:	B-2/12, Samruddhi Society, B, Parulekar Marg, Dadar. Mumbai-400028

Tel	:	022-24915071,24915073
Web	:	nawindia@vsnl.com
Contact person	:	Director
Summary of purpose	:	www.makeawish.indo.net

50. MANCHERJI EDULJI JOSHI MEMORIAL TRUST

Address	:	Jesia Bldg., Tame Jamshed Road, Parsi Colony, Mumbai-400014

51. MANECKJI AND SHIRINBAI NETERWALLA FOUNDATION

Address	:	Dai-Ichi Karkaria Pvt. Ltd., Liberty Bldg., Near Liberty Cinema, Sir Vithaldas Thakersey Marg, Maharashtra
Tel	:	2.2017130

52. MODI FOUNDATION

Address	:	Nirlon House, 2nd Floor, Dr. Annie Besant Road, Worli. Mumbai-400025
Tel	:	91-22-56637373
E-mail	:	administrator@modi.com
Web	:	www.modi.com
Contact person	:	Mrs. Veena Modi

53. N.M. WADIA CHARITIES

Address	:	123. M.G. Road, Murnbai-400023, Maharashtra

54. N.M. PETIT CHARITY FUND

Address	:	UCO Bank Bldg., 355/359, D.N. Road, Fort, Mumbai-400 001

55. NALANDA FOUNDATION

Address	:	4th Floor, Mahindra Towers, Dr. G.M. Bhosale Marg., Worli, Mumbai-400018
Tel	:	022-24935127/24964353
E-mail	:	feedback@schoolnet foundation.org
Web	:	www.nalandafoundation.org
Contact person	:	Mr. Anirdya Mukerji

56. NARAYANI GULAB FOUNDATION

Address	:	44, Vaikunth Chs, Lallubhai Park, Andheri (W), Mumbai400058, Maharashtra r
Contact person	:	Mr. Ramesh Kacholia

57. NAROTAM SEKHSARIA FOUNDATION

Address	:	122, Maker Chambers-III, Nariman Point, Mumbai-400021,
Tel	:	91-22-55597312
Web	:	www.nsscholarshi.net
Contact person	:	Dr, Seema Singh Ghosh

58. PARAGON CHARITABLE TRUST

Address	:	C/o. Paragon Textile Mills Ltd., P.B. Marg, Mumbai-400013
Tel	:	022-24938752/24938599
E-mail	:	trust@usa.net
Contact person	:	Ms. Rachna J. Adsule, Social Welfare Executive
Summary of purpose	:	Working in the areas of Health and Education and supporting projects which are sustainable in nature and have a social relevance
Subject Covered	:	Arts and Humanities, Education, Medicine and Health
Method of Activity	:	Self conducted programmes and grants to other
Priority of Interest	:	Victims of crime and corruption

59. RAJMUDRA FOUNDATION

Address	:	87, Atur House, Dr. A.B. Road, Worli, Mumbai-400018
Tel	:	022-24978075 / 76
E-mail	:	info@rajmudra.org
Contact person	:	Ms. Shalaka Patankar

60. RAJNI PATEL FOUNDATION

Address	:	C/o. Neo-Indcom Consultancy Pvt. Ltd., K-2, Cuffe Castle, Cuffe Parade, Mumbai-400005, Maharashtra
Contact person	:	Ms. Bakul Patel

61. RAMSARAN OBEROI CHARITABLE TRUST

Address	:	16, Sudesh, 2nd Floor, 17th Road, Opp Gurudwara Santa Cruz (W), Mumbai-400054, Maharashtra
Tel	:	022-26148320/26603235
Contact person	:	Dr. C.R. Oberoi, Managing Trustee

Summary of purpose : Grantmaking to institutions, grants to individuals, scholarships and fellowships etc. prizes
Subject Covered : Medicine and Health, Social Welfare and Social Studies
Method of Activity : Grants to others, grant making to institutions and grants to individuals, scholarships and fellowships
Priority of Interest : Children/Street Children, women, Aged, disabled.

62. RAVINDRA PATNI CHARITABLE TRUST
Address : 303/304, Regent Chambers, Nariman Point, Mumbai-400021,
Tel : 022-22873981/22822621
Contact person : Mr. Shailesh Patei

63. ROYAL COMMONWEALTH SOCIETY I'S' FOR THE BLIND
Address : South Asia Regional Office, B1/B3, Second Floor, Matru Ashish Jagmohandas Marg, 454, Nepean Sea Road, Mumbai-400 036

64. SADBHAV FOUNDATION
Address : Kayda Sahay Kendra, 2, Kayda Sahay Kendra, 2, Fort, Mumbai
Tel : 022-22621951
Contact person : Mr. Anil Kamdar
Method of Activity : Institutions for welfare of women

65. SAI SANSTHAN MARA KALI MEDICAL TRUST
Address : Maha Kali Road, Andheri East, Mumbai, Maharashtra
Contact person : Director
Subject Covered : Education, Medicine and Health
Method of Activity : Self Conducted programmes, scholarships, fellowships, prizes and training courses
Priority of Interest : Children/Street Children, Women and Aged

66. SAKAL INDIA FOUNDATION
Address : Sakal Building, 595, Budhwar Peth, Pune-411002

Tel : 24405500,/24035500/24455500
E-mail : indiafoundation@esakal.com
Web : www.eskal.com
Contact person : Executive Secretary

67. SANJIVANI TRUST
Address : Everest, A/1, 2nd Floor, 156, Tardeo Road, Tardeo, Mumbai-400034
Tel : 022-23512022/2352337
E-mail : sanjivani69@hotmail.com
Web : www.sanjivani.homestead.com
Contact person : Mr. H.C. Mehta. Trustee
Summary of purpose : Funds are given for mainly medical and education welfare of the poor needy irrespective of caste, creed and religion.
Method of Activity : Research, grants to institutions and individuals; scholarships, fellowships and prizes

68. SHAHANI TRUST
Address : 5-A, Court Chamber, 35, New Marine Lines, Mumbai-400020
Tel : 022-2004437,2001895
Contact person : Mr. Narayan Shahani

69. SHAPOORJEE PALLONJEE TRUST
Address : S.P. Centre, Near Fariyas Hotel, Minoo Desai Road, Colaba, Mumbai-400005
Tel : 22871040

70. SHIRINBAI SORABJI KHARAS CHARITABLE TRUST
Address : 303/4, Jupiter Apartments, Cuffe Parade, Mumbai-400005
Contact person : Mrs. Bhikoo Kharas
Summary of purpose : To open Hospitals and arrange Education for Common Men/Women, to give Financial help, to manage Libraries and Reading Rooms, to assist and support helpless persons during an emergency, to help those crippled or those otherwise in pain

71. SIR DORABJI TATAI TRUST
Address : Bombay House, 24, Homi Mody Street, Mumbai-400001

Tel	:	022-22049131
E-mail	:	snbatliwalla@tata.com / vkkarkaria@tata.com
Web	:	www.srtt.org
Contact person	:	Mr. S.N. Batliwalla

72. SIR HORMAZJI MODI TRUST OF HONGKONG

Address	:	C/o. Mrs. Nani N, Palkhiwala, Commonwealth Building, 6th Floor, Opp. Air India Bldg., Backbay Reclamation, Mumbai- 400021
Tel	:	22021184

73. SIR RATAN TATA TRUST

Address	:	Bombay House, 24, Homi Mody Street, Fort, Mumbai-400001
Tel	:	022-56658282
E-m all	:	srtt@tata.com
Web	:	www.srtt.org
Contact person	:	Mr. H.D. Malesra, Secretary & Chief Accountant
Summary of purpose	:	The Trust seeks to be a catalyst in development through giving grants to institutions in the areas of Rural Livelihoods and Communities, Education, Enhancing Civil society & Governance, Health and Arts & Culture. It also provides grants for endowments; has a separate programme for Small Grants and gives grants to individuals for education and medical relief.
Subject Covered	:	Within rural Livelihoods and communities, the Trust focuses on key initiatives within two borad areas: Land and water development. Microfinance.

74. SIR SHAPURJI BILLIMORIA FOUNDATION

Address	:	C/o. HDFC Bank, Ramon House, H.T. Parekh Marg, 169, Backbay Reclamation, Churchgate, Mumbai-400020
Tel	:	022-56316430

E-mail : delnazp@hdfcindia.com
Web : www.hdfc.com
Contact person : Ms. Delnaz Paliwalla

75. SOMANI PRATISHTHAN
Address : 135, Akshay Complex, Dhole Patil Road, Pune -411001
Tel : 020-26121372/26125199
E-mail : hitendra@giaspn01.vsnl.net.in
Contact person : Mr. Hitendra J. Somani, Trustee
Summary of purpose : To develop & promote Indian Art, Culture & Education by Lit way of developing youth
Subject Covered : Arts and Humanities, Education and International Affairs, youth development
Method of Activity : Self conducted programmes, Research, Prizes, Conferences, Seminars. Training and Publication
Priority of Interest : Children, Street Children, Youth & Adolescent

76. SUJATA CHARITY TRUST
Address : Industry House, 159, Churchgate Reclamation, Mumbai -400020
Tel : 022-2026340
Contact person : Mr. K.P. Chokhani
Subject Covered : Rural Development, Medicine and Health, STDs/AIDS, Research
Method of Activity : Publications to promote awareness and knowledge of these fields
Priority of Interest : Aged, Widows, Women, Children, Street Children, Tribals, SC/STs & OBCs

77. TATA CHEM GOLDEN JUBILEE FOUNDATION
Address : Bombay House, Sir Homi Mody Street, Fort. Mumbai-400023

78. TATA MEMORIAL SOCIAL SERVICE CENTRE
Address : Dr. E. Borges Road. Parel, Mumbai-400012, Maharashtra
Tel : 91-22-24177000, 24146750-55
E-mail : info@tmcmail.org / tmcitl@vsnl.com

Contact person	:	Mr. Patil (Chief MSW)
Subject Covered	:	Research and maritime studies
Method of Activity	:	Publications, self-conducted programmes, research, grants to institutions & individuals, scholarships, fellowships & training courses
Priority of Interest	:	Those interested in maritime studies

79. THE BRIDGE PUBLIC CHARITABLE TRUST

Address	:	Oasisi, Nehru Road, Vakola Santa Cruz (E), Mumbai-400029
Tel	:	022-26949955
E-mail	:	bridgetrust@vsnl.net
Web	:	www.bridgetrust.org
Contact person	:	Mr. J.M. Mehta

80. THE GOKAK MILLS CHARITABLE TRUST

Address	:	Forbes Building, Charanjit Rai Marg, Fort, Mumbai-400001
Contact person	:	Mr. K.C. Mehra

81. THE LOTUS TRUST

Address	:	510, Lotus House, V. Thacker C. Marg, New Marine Lines, Mumbai
Tel	:	022-22034279

82. THE SOONABAI PIROJSHA GODREJ FOUNDATION

Address	:	Godrej Industries Ltd., Pirojshanagar; Eastern Express Highway, Vikhroli (E), Mumbai-400079
Tel	:	(91-22) 25188010/25188020/25188030
Web	:	www.godrejindia.com
Contact person	:	Mr. A.B. Godrej

83. V.B. HARIBHAKTI CHARITABLE TRUST

Address	:	51, Maker Tower 'B', Cuffe Parade, Mumbai-400005
Contact person	:	Mr. V.B. Haribhakti

84. VADILAL GANDHI FOUNDATION

Address	:	Preadeep Nivas, Navroji Cross lane, Ghatkopar (W), Mumbai-400086
Tel	:	25153192
Contact person	:	Mr. Harish Gandhi

85. VAISHNOMAL MALHOTRA PUBLIC TRUST

Address	:	1/8-B, Ganga Estate, Behind Atur Park, Sion Trombay Road, Chembur, Mumbai-400071, Maharashtra
Tel	:	5564311
E-mail	:	chandramohan_nair@ril.com
Contact person	:	Mr. Chandra Mohan Nair, Secretary
Summary of purpose	:	Promotion of Rural Development and Educational Excellence
Subject Covered	:	Education and Rural Development
Method of Activity	:	Grant making
Priority of Interest	:	Rural people and students

86. VASANT J. SETH MEMORIAL FOUNDATION

Address	:	C/o. the Grat Eastern Shippiant Co. Ltd., Energy House, 81, D.N. Road, Mumbai-400001, Maharashtra
Tel	:	22677373/56352284
E-mail	:	Valerie_bocarro@greatship.com
Contact person	:	Ms. Asha Sheth
Summary of purpose	:	To promote better understanding of shipping, ship building and other maritime fields
Subject Covered	:	Education
Method of Activity	:	Self-conducted programmes and grants to others
Priority of Interest	:	Deserving and needy students

87. WADHWANI FOUNDATION

Address	:	2, Bina Apartments, Ground Floor, Guru Gangeshwar Marg, 6th Road, Khar (W), Mumbai-400052, Maharashtra
Tel	:	022-26006158
E-mail	:	info@wadhwani-foundation.org, divya@wadhwani-foundation.org
Web	:	www. wadhwani-foundation.org
Contact person	:	Ms. Divya Singh Gurbuxani, Programme Manager

88. WORLD ZOROASTRIAN ORGANISATION

Address	:	Shanti, 5th Floor, 6, Banaji Street, Mumbai-400001, Maharashtra

Tel	:	2283713

89. Y.C.Z.A. EDUCATIONAL & CHARITABLE TRUST

Address	:	Central Bank Bldg., Homi Mody Street, Fort, Mumbai-40002

90. Y.C.Z.A. EDUCATIONAL & CHARITABLE FUND

Address	:	R-11, 3rd Floor, Central Bank Bldg., Sir Homi Mody Street, Fort, Mumbai-400023, Maharashtra
Tel	:	2653075, 2654697
Contact person	:	Prof. N.A. Modi, Prof. K.C. Sheriar, Mr. D.E. Tata, Mr. B.S. Bhesania, Trustees
Summary of purpose	:	Deserving and needy students are given felloships and scholarships
Subject Covered	:	Rural development, Education, Social Welfare and Social Studies
Method of Activity	:	Grants to institutions and individuals, scholarships, fellowships and prizes
Priority of Interest	:	Women and Children

91. ZONTA CLUB OF BOMBAY

Address	:	Hardinge House, Gowalia Tank, Mumbai-400036 36, Maharashtra
Tel	:	022-3864248/3887815
Contact person	:	Dr. K. Madon
Summary of purpose	:	To promote health., education and economic welfare among women and children

Rajasthan

1. BHORUKA CHARITABLE TRUST

Address	:	VPO Bhorugram Block Rajgarh, (Sadulpur), Churu Distt.331035
Tel	:	0141-581431-34
E-mail	:	iihmr@iihmr.org
Contact person	:	Dr. Ashok Agarwal
Summary of purpose	:	Dedicated to socio-economic transformation of rural and remote areas of Churu District of Rajasthan through physical, social, cultural & economic development; implementing projects on health, education, natural

	resource management, sanitation, housing & income-generation activities in 250 villages of Rajgarh and Taranagar blocks of Churu District.

2. MAHARANA OF MEWAR CHARITABLE FOUNDATION

Address	: City Palace, Udaipur-313001, Rajasthan
Tel	: 294-241-9021/2/3/4/5/6/7/8/9
E-mail	: trusts@udaipur.hrindia.com
Web	: www.mewarindia.com/ noncomm/ public/mmcf.html

3. P.D. AGGARWAL FOUNDATION

Address	: 1, Prabhu Dayal Marg, Sanganer Airport, Jaipur-302001, Rajasthan
Tel	: 2560700%2561698
E-mail	: root@ihmrj. smetd.ernet.in
Contact person	: Mr. Ashok Aggarwal

4. URMUL TRUST

Address	: Urmul Bhawan, POB-55, Distt: Bikaner-334001, Rajasthan
Tel	: 0151-2523093,2522139
E-mail	: arvindojha @urmul.org, urmultrust@rediffmail.com
Contact person	: Mr. Arvind Ojha, Secretary

Tamil Nadu

1. A.M.M. FOUNDATION

Address	: "Parry House", 3rd Floor; 43, Moree Street, Chennai-600001
Tel	: 25340703/25341513
E-mail	: support@ammfoundation.org
Contact person	: Mr. M.V. Murugappan, Managing Trustee
Summary of purpose	: To establish hospitals, nursing homes, maternity and child care homes and other medical institutions for the aged
Subject Covered	: Arts and Humanities, Rural Development, Education, Medicine and Health, Social Welfare, Social Studies and Research

Method of Activity	:	Self-conducted programmes, grants to institutions and Individuals
Priority of Interest	:	Widows, Women, Children, Street Children, SC/STs, OBCs

2. AIDS PREVENTION AND CONTROL (APAC)

Address	:	Voluntary Health Services, Adyar, Chennai-600113, Tamil Nadu
Tel	:	044-22.541965/22541048
E-mail	:	apacvhs@vsnl.net
Contact person	:	Mr, Bimal Charles, Project Director
Summary of purpose	:	To help in the prevention of STDs by providing financial and technical assistance to NGOs
Subject Covered	:	Medicine and Health, STDs, AIDS
Method of Activity	:	Publications, self-conducted programmes, research, grants to institutions, conferences and training courses
Priority of Interest	:	Sex Workers and Other STD affected groups

3. AWERD-ASSOCIATION FOR WOMEN, EDUCATION AND RURAL DEVELOPMENT

Address	:	20/9, C-3, Blearathiyar Street, Arani-632301, TVM District
Tel	:	04173-25432

4. C.P RAMASWAMI AIYAR FOUNDATION

Address	:	The Grove, No. 1, Eldams Road, Chennai-600018, Tamil Nadu
Tel	:	044-24341778/24320756/24359022
E-mail	:	cprec@vsnl.com
Contact person	:	Dr. Nandita Krishna
Summary of purpose	:	To provide service based activities in education including running a school for children and those with learning disabilities, an education centre for environment
Subject Covered	:	Conservation and the Environment, Education, Social Welfare and Social Studies, Research

Method of Activity	:	Publications, self-conducted programmes, research, scholarships, fellowships and training courses
Priority of Interest	:	Children, Street Children, Women and Sex workers

5. CAN STOP

Address	:	Sundaram Medical Foundation, IV-Avenue, Shanthi Colony, Anna Nagar West, Chennai-600040
Tel	:	044-26284256
E-mail	:	canstop@vsnl.com
Web	:	www.canstop.org
Contact person	:	Dr. Vijaya Bharathi Rangarajan

6. CERYAC TRUST

Address	:	7, 18th East Street, Kamraj Nagar, Chennai-600041, Tamil Nadu
Tel	:	24490229/24490144
E-mail	:	ceyrac@md3.vsnl.net.in
Contact person	:	Mr. R.S. Kannan / Mr. Shankar
Summary of purpose	:	To run a primary school for rural children, free health centres. a tailoring unit and alternative employment schemes (eg. petty shops)
Subject Covered	:	Rural Development, Economic Affairs, Education, Medicine and Health, Social Welfare and Social Studies
Method of Activity	:	Self-conducted programmes, grants to institutions and individuals and training courses

7. DAMIEN FOUNDATION INDIA TRUST

Address	:	14, Venugopal Avenue, Spurtank Road, Chetpet. Chennai600031
Tel	:	0091-44-28360496/28361910
E-mail	:	damienin@vsnl.com
Contact person	:	Dr. P. Krishnamurthy, Secretary
Summary of purpose	:	Leprosy & TB Control
Method of Activity	:	Self-conducted programmes; Leprosy eradication and TB control
Geographical Scope	:	Entire Community

8. ILAIGNARKAL EDUCATION CENTRE AUROVILLE FOUNDATION

Address	:	Matrimandir- West, Auroville-605101, Tamil Nadu
Tel	:	0413-2622037
E-mail	:	'tamil@auroville.org.in
Web	:	www.auroville.org.in
Contact person	:	Prof. R. Meenakshi

9. INDIAN CULTURAL RESEARCH TRUST

Address	:	2nd Floor, Rajah Muthiah Hall, Rukmani Lakshmipathi Road, Egmore, Chennai-600008, Tamil Nadu
Tel	:	28554690
Contact person	:	Mr. Varadan
Summary of purpose	:	To fund activities in the field of culture and social welfare centres, a tailoring unit and alternative employment schemes (eg. petty shops)
Subject Covered	:	Social Welfare and Social Studies

10. JAAN CHARITABLE TRUST

Address	:	3rd Floor, 303, Anna Salai, Teynampet, Chennai-600035, Tamil Nadu
Tel	:	044-2453988
Contact person	:	Mr. Tara Rao
Summary of purpose	:	To provide assistance in cash and kind for people and institutions involved in animal protection and animal care
Subject Covered	:	Medicine and Health, Social Welfare and Social Studies. Animal Care
Method of Activity	:	Self-conducted programmes and grants to institutions
Priority of Interest	:	People and institutions involved in Animal Protection and Animal Care

11. KARNA PRAYAG TRUST (WELFARE CENTRE FOR WOMEN AND CHILDREN)

Address	:	7, Raja Krishna Rao Road, Teynampet, Chennai-600018, Tamil Nadu
Tel	:	044-24355182
Contact person	:	Administrative Officer

12. KOVAI HEART FOUNDATION

Address	:	154, Bharathi Colony, Peelamedu, Coimbatore-641004, Tamil Nadu
Tel	:	0422-2567567, 2566566
E-mail	:	balasundaram@kovaiheartfoundation.org
Web	:	www.kovaiheartfoundation.org
Contact person	:	Dr. S. Balasundaram
Summary of purpose	:	To help prevent Heart and Lung Diseases by creating public awareness. To help poor patients undergo treatment at concessional rates. To perform Open Heart Surgery for indigent patients at concessional rates or free of cost.

13. KRISHNA IYER'S CHARITABLE TRUST

Address	:	14, Chinniah Road, T. Nagar, Chennai-600017, Tamil Nadu
Contact person	:	Mr. V. Nilakantan
Summary of purpose	:	To provide financial aid for education
Subject Covered	:	Education
Method of Activity	:	Grants to individuals
Priority of Interest	:	Students

14. KSR EDUCATIONAL AND CHARITABLE TRUST

Address	:	KSR Kalvi Nagar, Namakkal District, Tiruchengode-637209
Tel	:	04288-274741 to 44
E-mail	:	ksrct@md2.vsnl.net.in
Web	:	www.ksr.edu
Contact person	:	Dr. K.S. Rangasamy, MJF

15. KUMARAPPA NATIONAL MEMORIAL TRUST

Address	:	131/78, San Thome High Road, Chennai-600004, 'Tamil Nadu
Tel	:	24940967/24942430
Contact person	:	Mr. N.S. Ranganathan
Summary of purpose :	:	To promote research, training and involvement of youth and women in rural development, conservation of environment, non-renewable energy resources, Khadi and village industries,

		basic education, publication of Gandhian literature
Subject Covered	:	Rural development, Conservation, Environment, Education, Research
Method of Activity	:	Publications, Research, Grants to institutions
Priority of Interest	:	People or institutions involved in promoting Gandhian values

16. LADIES CIRCLE NO. 38

Address	:	Gee Cee Villa, 2nd Street, Poes Garden, Kasturi Rangan Road, Chennai-600086, Tamil Nadu
Tel	:	4993097
Contact person	:	Ms. Archana Duseja
Summary of purpose	:	To run a children's home, provide donations in kind such as sewing machines, calipers and other equipment
Subject Covered	:	Education, Medicine and Health, Social Welfare and Social Studies
Method of Activity	:	Self-conducted programmes and grants to individuals
Priority of Interest	:	Widows, Women, Children, Street Children and Slum dwellers

17. LADIES CIRCLE NO. 62

Address	:	9, Subba Rao Avenue, 1st Street, Nungambakkam, Chennai-600006, Tamil Nadu
Tel	:	28276110
Contact person	:	Ms. Alia Sharma
Summary of purpose	:	To help orphans and destitutes in cash and kind
Sunject Covered	:	Economic Affairs; Medicine and Health
Method of Activity	:	Self-conducted programmes and grants to others
Priority of Interest	:	Children, Street Children and Slum dwellers

18. LADIES CIRCLE NO. 7

Address	:	75, Sriram Colony, Abhiramapuram, Chennai-600018, Tamil Nadu

Tel	:	24970265
Contact person	:	Ms. Tara Shyam
Summary of purpose	:	To provide education for children, engage specialists (speech therapists) to work in schools. provide donations in cash and kind and ran old age homes
Subject Covered	:	Education, Social Welfare and Social Studies
Method of Activity	:	Self-conducted programmes, grants to institutions and Individuals
Priority of Interest	:	Aged, Children, Street Children and Slum dwellers

19. LION DISTRICT CENTRAL OFFICE 324 Al

Address	:	Bagirama Residency, 124, Marshall Road, Egmore, Chennai600008
Contact person	:	Lion Lakshimpathy. (District Governor)
primary of purpose	:	To provide educational and medical assistance (cataract surgery) surgery)
Subject Covered	:	Education, Medicine and Health, Social Welfare and Social Studies
Method of Activity	:	Publications, self-conducted programmes, grants to institutions and individuals, scholarships and fellowships

20. MAC/ACM TRUST AND FOUNDATION

Address	:	MAC/IHC Building, VHS Campus, T.T.T.I. Post, Chennai-600113, Tamil Nadu
Tel	:	2541176 76
E-mail	:	vtdoss@md4.vsnl.net
Contact person	:	V. Thulsi Doss

21. MADRAS CRAFT FOUNDATION

Address	:	G-3. Madhuram Flats, No. 6. Urur Olcott Road, Besant Nagar, Chennai-600090, Tamil Nadu
Tel	:	044-24462435
mail	:	mcfdak@md3.vsnl.net.in
Web	:	www.dakshinachitra.org
Contact person	:	Vishalam Ramanathan

Summary of purpose : The preservation and promotion of the arts, crafts and architecture of South India

22. MEENAKSHI MISSION HOSPITAL AND RESEARCH CENTRE (MMHRC), (RUN BY S.R. TRUST)

Address : Lake Area, Melur Road, Madurai-625107, Tamil Nadu
Tel : 0091-452-2588741 (10 lines)
F-mail : mmhrc@sancharnet, inmmhre@eth.net
Web : www.meenakshimission.org
Contact person : Dr. N. Sethuraman

23. MONDAY CHARITY CLUB

Address : 1, Sapthagiri Apartment, 83, T.T.K. Salai, Chennai-600018
Tel : 24996634
Contact person : Ms. Savithri Vaidhi
Priority of Interest : Widows, Women, Children, Street Children and other economically backward groups

24. MOTHER THERESA WOMEN'S EDUCATION AND DEVELOPMENT SOCIETY

Address : 27, Vellore Road, Polur-606803, Tamil Nadu
Contact person : The Executive Director

25. NANDINI VOICE FOR THE DEPR IVED

Address : M-60/1, 4th Cross Street, Besant Nagar, Chennai-600090
Tel : 91-44-24961346/24961792
E-mail : nsvenkat@md4.vsnl.net.in
Web : www. nandinivoive.tripod.com
Contact person : Mr. N. S. Venkataraman

26. NAWAB WELFARE ASSOCIATION

Contact person : Ms. Nagmani
Summary of purpose : Advocacy for the welfare of the handicapped, financial assistance for education and women's development
Subject Covered : Education, Medicine and health, Social Welfare and Social Studies
Method of Activity : Grants to individuals

Priority of Interest : Widows, Women, Street children and physically handicapped

27. NEW LIFE CHARITABLE TRUST

Address : No.31/50, Sai Park Periyazhwar Street, Sundaram Colony East Tambaram, Chennai-600059, Tamil Nadu

Tel : 22399551

Summary of purpose : Old & Helpless children

28. ORCHID TRUST

Address : 4th Floor, 'Crown Court' No. 128 (Old No. 34), Cathedral Road, Chennai-600086, Tamil Nadu

Tel : 91-44-28110914

E-mail : orchidtrust@orchidpharma.com

Summary of purpose : The key thrust areas that the Orchid Trust works on are Education, Health, Self-employment, Capacity building, Community Asset Development and Youth development. The Trust has adopted 12 villages and 5 Panchayats and works continuously in implementing several welfare schemes in its identified thrust areas.

29, RAJESHWARI NATHAN FOUNDATION

Address : 13, West Road, CIT Nagar (W), Chennai-600035, Tamil Nadu

Contact person : Mr. Nathan S.K.

Summary of purpose : To provide grants for education to youth from poor backgrounds and for health related problems

Subject Covered : Education, Medicine and health

Method of Activity : Grants to individuals; scholarships and fellowships

Priority of Interest : Children and Street Children

30. RANGAMMAL GOPALACHARI TRUST

Address : AB-51, Second Street, Anna Nagar, Chennai-600040, Tamil Nadu

Tel : 044-26285369

E-mail : rgt@rediffmail.com

Contact person : Mr. Ravi Natarajan

31. RATHNA & RAO WISDOM TRUST

Address	:	17 (old N o.9), Desika Road, Chennai-600004, Tamil Nadu
Tel	:	2499032'7
Contact person	:	Dr. K.V. Govinda Rao, Managing Trustee
Method of Activity	:	The income derived from our investments is being spent to help deaf, dumb, blind and handicapped citizens besides helping poor students

32. RELIEF FOUNDATION

Address	:	New No. 18, Old No.30, Shreeram Nagar, Thiruvanmiyur, Chennai-600041, Tamil Nadu
Tel	:	24916854

33. ROTARY NEWS TRUST

Address	:	Dugar Towers, 3rd Floor, 34 Marshalls Road, Egmore, Chennai600008
Tel	:	044-28528818/52147094
E-mail	:	kvchari@rosaonline.org
Web	:	www.rosaonline.org
Contact person	:	Mr. Krishan V. Chari
Summary of purpose	:	Service to community
Priority of Interest	:	Socially deprived

34. ROUND TABLE 3 CHILD EDUCATION TRUST

Address	:	6, Casa Major Road. Chennai-600008, Tamil Nadu
Tel	:	044-28194651
E-mail	:	nairanil@vsnl.com
Contact person	:	Mr. Anil Nayar

35. ROUND TABLE FOUNDATION

Address	:	No.80, Nungambakkam High Road. Chennai-600034. Tamil Nadu
Tel	:	28274539
Contact person	:	Mr. A. Sridharan
Summary of purpose	:	To support poor communities with education, medical care and shelter
Method of Activity	:	Rural development, Conservation and Environment, Education, Medicine and

Health. Social Welfare and Social Studies

interest : Aged, Children, Street Children, Women, Sex Workers and Other Backward Castes

36. SAMAYA SWEEKRUTA TRUST

Address : 4/1, 3rd Street Shantiniketan Colony, Madambakkam, Tambaram, Chennai, Tamil Nadu

Tel : 2274478

37. SHRIRAM SOCIAL WELFARE TRUST

Address : No.9, Seethamai Colony, III Main Road, Alwarpet, Chennai600018

Tel : 24341151

Summary of purpose : Ashram Home for Street Children

38. SRI ADISHANKARA KAMAKSHI EDUCATION TRUST

Address : Shanmugananda Koil, Mangadu, Chennai-600101, Tamil Nadu

Tel : 26493151

39. SRI RAM EDUCATIONAL. TRUST

Address : 18, Evening Bazar Road, Chennai-600003, Tamil Nadu

Tel : 25350580

Contact person : Mr. Devraj Naidu

Summary of purpose : To provide financial aid to children, runs a polytechnic, an engineering college and an arts and science college

Method of Activity : Grants to individuals

Priority of Interest : Children and Street Children

40. SRI V. NARAYANA IYER MEMORIAL TRUST

Address : Gitalaya. Block-AD-48, Anna Nagar, Chennai-600040, Tamil Nadu

Tel : 26213504/26212454

E-mail : voswanat@md3.vsnl.net.in

Contact person : Mr. Narayana Vishwanath

Summary of purpose : To help the needy to inculcate a sense of 'Bhakti' and organize Annadanams i.e. donations

Subject Covered : Social Welfare and Social Studies

Method of Activity	:	Self conducted programmes and grants to others

41. SRI VUPPUTUR ALWAR CHETTY CHARITIES

Address	:	183, Govındappa Naichan Street, Chennai-600001, Tamil Nadu
Tel	:	25222447/25380661
Contact person	:	Mr. V. Ananda Krishna Chetty
Summary of purpose	:	The Trust focuses only on educational activities
Subject Covered	:	Education
Method of Activity	:	Grants to individuals

42. SRI POORNA MAHAMERU TRUST

Address	:	Sankara Salai, Suham Nagar, Old Pallavaram, Chennai-600059, Tamil Nadu
Tel	:	22472483

43. ST. GEORGE CHARITABLE TRUST

Address	:	Stardrive Busducts P. Ltd., 5, Smith Road, Chennai-600002
Tel	:	044-8522425'8522208
E-mail	:	stardriv@satyam.net.in
Contact person	:	Mr. K.L. Thadani
Summary of purpose	:	Basically an educational trust to support children
Subject Covered	:	Education
Method of Activity	:	Grants to individuals
Priority of Interest	:	Children and Street Children

44. SUBBIAH DHARAIANIDHI

Address	:	Annamalai College Campus, Tiruchendur Road, Tuticorin28003
Tel	:	0461-332925 & 0422-214835
E-mail	:	acew@vsnl.com
Contact person	:	Shri D. Ganesan, Managing Trustee
Summary of purpose	:	Education with emphasis for women
Subject Covered	:	Education, Medicine & Health, Rural Development, Social Welfare and Social Studies Self conducted programmes, Grants to institutions and individuals, scholarships, fellowships, prizes,

		conferences, training & publications and Children

45. SUKRITI CHARITABLE TRUST

Address	:	No. 13 MGR Road, Kalakshetra Colony Besant Nagar, Chennai 600090
Tel	:	24919447

46. SUNDARAM MEDICAL FOUNDATION

Address	:	Dr. Rangarajan Memorial Hospital, Shanthi Colony, IV Avenue, Anna Nagar, Chennai-600040, Tamil Nadu
Tel	:	(91)-(044)-26268844
E-mail	:	ravindran_sri@rediffmail.com
Web	:	www.smfhospital.org
Contact person	:	Mr. S. Ravindran

47. TANKER FOUNDATION

Address	:	10, Wheatcrofts Road, Nungambakkam, Chennai-600 034, Tamil Nadu
Tel	:	91-44-28273407/28258455
E-mail	:	tankerfoundation@rediffmail.com
Web	:	www.help4help.net
Contact person	:	Ms. Latha Kumaraswami
Subject Covered	:	Medicine, Health and Research Welfare and Social Studies
Method of Activity	:	Self conducted programmes, research, grants to institutions and individuals, prizes and conferences
Priority of Interest	:	Aged, Children, Street Children, Women, Sex Workers, Tribals, SC/STs and Other Backward Castes

48. THE C.P. RAMASWAMI AIYER FOUNDATION

Address	:	No. l, Eldams Road, Alwarpet, Cheimai-600018, Tamil Nadu
Tel	:	044-24341778/24346526/24337023
E-mail	:	cpreec@vsnl.com
Web	:	cpreec.org
Contact person	:	The Director
Summary of purpose	:	Aim to provide quality education in an atmosphere congenial for the child to

		imbibe values and ideas and aim for excellence

49. V.S.S. JAIN TRUST

Address	:	77, Pillayar Koil Street, Chennai-600005. Tamil Nadu
Tel	:	28552245
Contact person	:	Mr. Dham Chand
Method of Activity	:	Grants to institutions & individuals, scholarships, fellowships & prizes

50. VALLIAMAL EDUCATIONAL TRUST

Address	:	E-9, Anna Nagar (E)., Chennai-600108, Tamil Nadu
Tel	:	91-44-26262816
Contact person	:	Mr. A.M. Pararnasivanandam
ubje,t Covered	:	Education
Method of Activity	:	Grants to individuals, scholarships and fellowships
Priority of Interest	:	Women

51. VAVILLA VENKATESWARA SASTRULA TRUST (VV S TRUST)

Address	:	26, Ramanuja Iyer Street, Chennai-600021, Tamil Nadu
Tel	:	25951378
Contact person	:	Mr. S. Swaminathan, Managing Trustee
Summary of purpose	:	Provide scholarships to poor students and impart knowledge of Vedas
Subject Covered	:	Education
Method of Activity	:	Self conducted programmes, scholarships and fellowships
Priority of Interest	:	Children and Street Children

52. VEI MISSION

Address	:	33, Radhakrishna Nagar, Chennai-600019, Tamil Nadu
Contact person	:	Mr. Prabhakar
Summary of purpose	:	To promote education, social welfare and rural development

53. VISHRANTHI CHARITABLE TRUST

Address	:	Vishranthi Home for Aged Destitute Women, 4/227, M.G.R. Salai,

		Palavakkam, Chennai-600041, Tamil Nadu
	Tel	: 044-24996634/24994806
	Contact person	: Mrs. Savithrivaithi
54.	VKK CHARITIES	
	Address	: 49, Thirumalai Pillai Road, T. Nagar, Chennai-600017, Tamil Nadu
	Tel	: 28277378
	Contact person	: Dr. P. Arivasagan
	Summary of purpose	: To provide educational aid and runs polytechnics
	Subject Covered	: Education, Medicine and Health
	Method of Activity	: Grants to institutions
	Priority of Interest	: Students
55.	WILLINGDON CHARITABLE TRUST	
	Address	: 3rd Floor, Rajah Muthiah Hall, Rukmani Lakshmipathy Road, Egmore, Chennai-600008, Tamil Nadu
56.	WORLD OF LIFF SERVICES	
	Address	: 15, village Road, 1st lane, Chennai-600034, Tamil Nadu
	Tel	: 2827527
	Contact person	: Mr. Koshy
	Summary of purpose	: To provide counselling for drug addicts. and sponsorships for the needy
	Subject Covered	: Counselling, spiritual activities, ref erral centre for donations
	Method of Actiyity	: Self conducted programmes
	Priority of Interest	: Widows, Women, Children, Street Children and Drug addicts
57.	WORLD UNIVERSITY SERVICES CENTRE	
	Address	: 18. East Spurtank Road Chennai-600031, Tamil Nadu
	Tel	: 28263991
	Contact person	: Prof. Bojappa
	Summary of purpose	: To conduct medical & health camps and run a hostel for students & teachers
	Subject Covered	: Education, Medicine and Health
	Method of Activity	: Self conducted programmes, scholarships and fellowships

Uttar Pradesh

1. HPS FOUNDATION

Address	:	Plot No.3, Sector-125 (G. Noida Expressway) Noida-201301
Tel	:	95120-2432750-79
E-mail	:	hps.foundation@hpsglobal. com/ hps.coundation@pstsi.com
Contact person	:	Mr. R.B. Vohra

2. ASHA FOR EDUCATION

Address	:	A-893, Indira Nagar, Lucknow-226016, Uttar Pradesh
Contact person	:	Mr. Voorakaranam
Summary of purpose	:	Funding primary education and literacy initiatives in India
Subject Covered	:	Education
Method of Activity	:	Through funding NGOs working in the field of education
Priority of Interest	:	Children (poor), street and working children, tribals

West Bengal

1. ANKUR LADIES CLUB AND WELFARE SOCIETY

Address	:	P-78, Lake Road, Kolkata-700029
Tel	:	033-24664542
E-mail	:	sblsen@vsnl.net
Contact person	:	Mrs. Krishna Sen
Summary of purpose	:	To provide assistance for different welfare activities specially on women.
Subject Covered	:	Economic Affairs. Education, Social Welfare and Social Studies, Organisations and individuals devoted to philanthropy.
Method of Activity	:	Grants to institutions and individuals.

2. BHORUKA PUBLIC WELFARE TRUST

Address	:	63, Rafi Ahmed Kidwai Road, Calcutta-700016
Tel	:	91-33-22448092/22174019
E-mail	:	bpwt@cal.vsnl.net.in / info@bpwt.org
Web	:	www.bhoruka.org/index.shtmll

Contact person	:	Dr. Asha Rao, Director
Summary of purpose	:	To provide health care services & building a sustainable society
Subject Covered	:	Behaviour change, communication, counselling, medical treatment including STDs, social marketing of condoms and developing peereducators
Method of Activity	:	Self-Conducted programmes, research, grants to institutions and individuals, scholarships and fellowships.
Priority of Interest	:	Poor rural people, Truck drivers and People suffering from medical problems such as STDs/AIDS.

3. CARE, WEST BENGAL

Address	:	12, Haralal Das Street, Calcutta-700014
Tel	:	2462840/2462843
E-mail	:	carewb@giasc101.vsnl.net.in
Web	:	www. careindia.org
Contact person	:	Ms. Nirrnala Gupta, State Director
Summary of purpose	:	Works for the betterment of the communities in India
Subject Covered	:	Integrated nutrition and health projects, promoting linkages for urban sustainable development, tribal empowerment, credit rotation for empowerment of women and primary education for girls.
Method of Activity	:	Grant making to organisations
Priority of Interest	:	Pregnant/lactating women and under two children, sex workers, industrial workers and their wives, and rural poor women living below the poverty line.

4. CHILD IN NEED INSTITUTE

Address	:	PO Pailan, Via Joka, Calcutta-700104
Tel	:	91 (033) 24978192/24978206
E-mail	:	cini@cinindia.org
Web	:	www.cini-india.org
Summary of purpose	:	To provide sustainable health and nutritional development for women and children

Subject Covered : Health care of children, women, street children, rehabilitation of Beverly malnourished children, women's empowerment, sexual health programmes for women and adolescents, programme for sexually abused children. research & promotion of communal harmony and international understanding

Method of Activity : Self conducted programme and grant making to institutions

Priority of interest : Vulnerable women and their under-five children in rural areas and urban slums, adolescent girls and women, street children/child Labour and sex workers and their clients.

5. CHILDREN'S AID CALCUTTA

Address : 52-A, Rabindranath Chowdhury Road, Calcutta-700015

Tel : 23291046.,23292024

E-mail : cac@cal.vsnl.net.in

Contact person : Fr. Joseph Cherian

Summary of purpose : To provide financial assistance to poor and needy children for their education and health care.

Subject Covered : Education, Health Care, Nutrition, Value Formation, Family Assistance, Poor and needy children

Method of Activity : Grants to children and institutions.

6. HINDUSTAN CHARITY TRUST

Address : 78, Syed Amir Ali Avenue, Calcutta-700019

Tel : 033-22471263

Contact person : Mr. S.N. Gupta

Summary of purpose : To establish and support schools, colleges, libraries, reading rooms, lecture halls, public museums and art galleries.

Subject Covered : Arts and Humanities, Rural Development, Education, Social

		Welfare and Social Studies SC/STs, Other Backward Castes and Women
Method of Activity	:	Grants to institutions and individuals, scholarships and fellowships,

7. NIRMAN (B.D. BANGUR ENDOWMENT)

Address	:	31, Chowringhee Road. Kolkata-700016
Tel	:	22265755 / 5547
mail	:	mail@bdbangur-endowment.com
Contact person	:	Indrani Chatterjee

8. SAHAY

Address	:	734, Block-P, New Alipur, Calcutta-700053
Tel	:	24005767 /2400576
E-mail	:	sahavci@cal.vsnl.net.in
Contact person :	:	Mr. Saradindu Banerjee
Summary of purpose	:	To provide financial aid and non financial support to grassroots organizations involved in child development programmes
Subject Covered	:	Education; Medicine and Health, Rural Development, Community Group Formation, Child Rights and the Environment
Method of Activity	:	Self-conducted programmes, grants to institutions and training courses.
Geographical Scope	;	Children from disadvantaged families and Street Children

9. SAMARPAN FOUNDATION

Address	:	Samarpan. 70-C, Prof. Suniti Chatterjee Street. Calcutta-700029 Tel
4641685/4640296		
E-mail	:	atma@gmcindia.com
Contact person	:	Mr. Atma Saraogi
Summary of purpose	:	To promote international welfare and upliftment of people in general also engaged in advancement of any object of public utility
Subject Covered	:	International Welfare, Upliftment of people, Education and Medical Relief

Method of Activity	:	Grant making to organizations and individuals

10. THE PAUL FOUNDATION

Address	:	15, Park Street, Kolkata-700016
Tel	:	033-22295455-8
E-mail	:	thepaulfoundation@apeejay.com
Web	:	www.thepaulfoundation.org
Summary of purpose	:	Scholarships

11. THE SEAGULL FOUNDATION FOR THE ARTS

Address	:	26, Circus Avenue, Calcutta-700017
Tel	:	033-2403636,2407942
E-mail	:	seagull@giasc101.vsnl.net.in
Contact person	:	Mr. Naveen Kishore
Summary of purpose	:	Visual arts and Translation project